IT'S A FREE COUNTRY!

*A Young Person's Guide
to Politics & Elections*

Two young volunteers hand out campaign literature for 1984 presidential candidate Senator John Glenn of Ohio. A former astronaut who looked like a winner, Glenn couldn't seem to capture the imagination of the voters, and he dropped out early in the race.

IT'S A FREE COUNTRY!

A Young Person's Guide

to Politics & Elections

by

CYNTHIA K.

SAMUELS

ATHENEUM   1988   New York

Copyright © 1988 by Cynthia K. Samuels

Atheneum
Macmillan Publishing Company
866 Third Avenue, New York, NY 10022
Collier Macmillan Canada, Inc.
First Edition
Typography by Mary Ahern
Printed in the United States of America
10 9 8 7 6 5 4 3 2 1

Library of Congress Cataloging-in-Publication Data

Samuels, Cynthia K.
It's a free country!: a young person's guide to politics and
elections/by Cynthia K. Samuels.—1st ed.
p. cm.
Bibliography: p. 124
Includes index.
Summary: Discusses the nature of politics in this country and the
way people get elected to office. Includes some case histories of
elected officials and tips for things you can do to participate in
campaigns and elections.
ISBN 0–689–31416–7
1. Elections—United States—Juvenile literature. 2. United
States—Politics and government—Juvenile literature.
[1. Elections. 2. Politics, Practical. 3. United States—Politics
and government.] I. Title.
JK1978.S25 1988
324.973—dc19   87–30857 CIP AC

*This book is dedicated
to my parents, who taught me to love politics,
to my husband, Rick, for loving it all with me
from the day we met and began our lifelong debate
about the right way to run the world,
and to our sons, Joshua and Daniel,
who are learning to make their own decisions
about how things should be.*

Acknowledgments

First of all, I would like to thank Robert Squier, who gave me the idea for this book. Like most of his ideas, it was a good one. I also want to thank the Class of '87 at the Ethical Culture School in New York City, whose interested questions and thoughtful opinions were the real inspiration for a book about politics. Special thanks to their social studies teacher, Liz Takoushian, whose comments have been so very helpful.

Thanks to Roan Conrad, who provided not only invaluable organizational suggestions, but also an endorsement of my efforts at a time when that sort of support was sorely needed.

Les Guthman took the time to review this book line by line and to make valuable and skillful suggestions. His care, and his enthusiasm, made a great deal of difference.

Editor Marcia Marshall has been a supportive and very creative force. Her enthusiasm as well as her wise and skillful comments have been invaluable.

Thanks go of course to my parents, Jeanne and Emerson Samuels, who, when I began a rock-star worship of John Kennedy, provided inauguration tickets and news magazine subscriptions instead of mere tolerance, and who always demanded that I offer not only political ideas and opinions but also evidence that I had thought them through before I acted on them.

To my high school history teacher, the late John Fleckenstein, go thanks for a provocative education I never appreciated until much later. To Richard Strojan, thanks for giving me the courage to call myself a writer, and the initial belief that I could live up to the name. To the Smith College American Studies department, thanks not only for rich training, but also for the openness to let me take off and work in politics and still earn my degree.

To Steve Friedman, former executive producer of "Today," thanks for letting me chase politicians around and call it work.

To Sylvia Westerman, Bill Small, and Roger Mudd, thanks for a wonderful start.

To Mrs. Naomi Robinson—thanks for friendship and support at all times in all ways.

Finally, to my husband, Richard Atkins, and my sons, Joshua and Daniel Atkins, go the greatest thanks. As long as I cared, so did they. Rick never lets me get away with less than my best at anything and is an intelligent and knowledgeable editor. He also tolerated interruptions of work, sleep, and meals when computer emergencies demanded his expert guidance. Josh and Daniel ask and listen, notice and observe. Everything they offer is intelligent and helpful. Politics is great, but if the guys in your life aren't with you—what's the point? Thanks, guys.

Contents

IT'S A FREE COUNTRY!

*A Young Person's Guide
to Politics & Elections*

Introduction

Story of a Winner

When state senator Robert Graham decided that he wanted to be governor of Florida, nobody thought he could do it. He was an *unknown,* and wasn't sure how to become familiar to the voters. Florida is a long and skinny state, and its cities are far apart. That means there are several sets of television stations; one station can't reach the whole state. So when you make commercials, as any *candidate* for governor must do, those commercials have to be shown in all those different *markets,* or selling regions. You have to buy separate television time for advertising in each area. As you can imagine, that costs a lot of money.

Graham's campaign advisors had a good idea though. If they couldn't buy all that air time, they could do something so interesting that people would put Graham on TV for free—because what he was doing was news. It would appeal to city people in Miami and to voters at the other end of the state as well. What they chose was an idea called "work days."

Each day, candidate Graham went out in the state of Florida and worked at a different job. He was a hospital orderly, a garbage collector, a waiter, even an equipment manager for the Miami Dolphins football team. What Flor-

1

ida people did for a living, Bob Graham did too. Soon everyone in the state was watching the news to see what Graham had done that day, and what he thought of their job. He didn't need TV commercials, he was real live news, fair and square.

He also became more acceptable in parts of the state where he hadn't been very popular, and enhanced his image throughout Florida. He won the election, but kept on doing work days through two terms as governor. In 1986, Governor Graham was elected to the United States Senate.

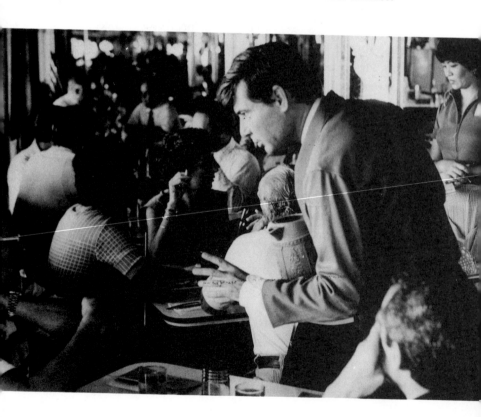

Bob Graham got the voters' attention by trying out different jobs. He did each job for a day and called his efforts "work days." Voters learned about Bob Graham by watching him work. Though he's a United States Senator now, he still does work days from time to time. (Bob Graham Senate Campaign)

When you watch your favorite baseball team, or see your favorite group on MTV, you like them better if you know something about them. Knowing a little bit about each of the Amazin' Mets, or that Huey Lewis loves to play golf and that's why he named one of his albums *Fore!*, can really help you to enjoy them more.

You may expect it to be boring to think about people running for office, especially if they aren't running for president. But think about this: movie star Clint Eastwood got elected mayor of a small town in California because lots of people didn't want fast-food restaurants messing up their charming little village.

In Long Island, New York, there was an elected town council that banned eating ice cream cones on the street. And there are towns in the United States where elected officials have banned rock music. So when you decide to ignore politics and to let other people pay attention to what's happening in your school or your town or your state or your country, you are letting yourself in for a lot of trouble, and you won't have any say in changing it.

If you watch television, you've seen commercials for people running for office. Serious or funny, they all have the same message: "Vote for me!" But what you see on TV, or even what you see when you meet a candidate walking around town and shaking hands with voters, is the smallest part of an operation as complicated and exciting as the design of a football play or the production of a music video. To know what's going on in politics, as people fight for the right to govern your city or town or country, you have to have some of the insider's view. That's what this book is about.

Chapter 1

What Is Politics, Anyway?

Underneath all the hoopla that gets a person elected is something very important: ideas about what government should or should not do. We vote for the people who have the same ideas about government that we do. If enough people agree, their candidate is elected.

Politics is the set of skills and methods candidates use to get elected to a job in government, and the art of keeping that job and managing it well once they have it.

Governing is what they do after they're elected. They use political skills though, to make their work easier, even after the election. And though you may not notice it, any time you work in a group, you are probably using politics, too.

Starting at the End

Since most of this book is about running for office, let's think first about what happens once you get the office—when the politics slows down a bit and the real work of government kicks in. Suppose you are elected to head up a school project. Six people on your committee want to do it one way, seven another. You have to work out an agreement that will keep the two groups from quarreling so much that nothing gets accomplished. That's the same thing a senate committee chairman or a president has to do; theirs is just a bigger, older group. All of you need political skills to keep the work moving and the voters happy.

For example, hammering out agreements is a political skill. In a democratic system, there is no way to run something without the approval of the people whose thing you are running, so you use the tools of the politician. You learn to get people to agree, or if they can't agree, to compromise. You learn how to convince people that their interest lies in the "big picture" and that it is worth giving up a little of what they want in order to get the big picture to happen. You also learn to do a little healthy *horse trading;* you give a little of this and they give a little of that and things get done. In short, you become a politician.

That also means that you try to find out if your administration—as class president, dance chairman, or captain of the basketball team—is doing things the way people want them to be done. If they don't like it, you have two choices: you can either change what you are doing, or convince them that your way is right.

Every politician has to do that, whether he or she is class president or president of the United States. Because if you are elected, and you want to get elected again, you have to be *accountable* to those who vote for you. If they don't like what you do, they will vote for someone else next time.

That Even Happens to Presidents

The most famous example is what happened to President Lyndon Johnson in the 1960s, during the United States' involvement in the war in Vietnam. Though several presidents share responsibility for that war, and for the American decision to keep sending soldiers to fight that very difficult "enemy" in Southeast Asia, only one president, Johnson, lost his job because of it. It was an example of the damage that politics, and the misinterpretation of what people want from their leaders, can cause.

President Lyndon Johnson had great dreams for the United States. A poor Texas boy, he was determined to lead the country into a "Great Society," where the poor and undereducated could have a better chance. And he might have done it. But he also believed, as did many of his generation, that the United States had a responsibility to stop communism wherever it appeared; to keep the world safe from what he saw as the evil of such a system. So as the Communist North Vietnamese moved harder and harder against the people of South Vietnam, Johnson decided, with encouragement from many very knowledgeable advisors, that the United States should send more soldiers and money and equipment to that small Southeast Asian country.

Young men in the United States were being drafted into the army to go to Vietnam. Some of them did not accept the idea of being drafted to go fight a war supporting a system that they saw as corrupt. Others just didn't want to go. Still others thought that Vietnam should decide its own fate. Some of their parents felt the same way.

Soon there were marches and demonstrations all over the United States. Some demonstrators chanted to Lyndon Johnson, "Hey, hey, LBJ, how many kids did you kill today?" These days that sounds pretty awful, but one reason the war caused such bitterness is that the United States was using a kind of chemical called napalm to bomb the country. Napalm would stick to your skin and catch fire when it hit. Many children got hit with it, since Vietnam was mostly little villages and pilots couldn't choose exactly where the napalm would land.

These children are running away from a napalm raid. The young girl in the center had been hit by napalm and had torn off her burning clothes. You can see why this photograph is one of the most famous photographs from the war in Vietnam. (Wide World Photos, Inc.)

In earlier times, most people didn't see the results of war unless they were soldiers. This war, though, was the first one in history to be fought on television. New videotape and satellite technology made it possible for all Americans to watch the war as it was being fought, as camera crews and reporters sent stories home to be shown on the evening news. Americans saw the napalm burns on TV. They also saw their young countrymen fighting, and often dying, right before their eyes. It was the first time *all* Americans could see how terrible war—any war—could be.

It also appeared to many that the United States was losing the war. Maybe all the TV drama would have mattered less if people had felt that there was a chance to win. But as the years went by and more and more Americans died, those who remained couldn't see any results. The country just seemed to be getting in deeper and, as more people complained, Johnson couldn't decide whether to commit everything we had, in an effort to win, or to slow down the war effort in order to please his opponents. That uncertainty added to the image of a country fighting a war of confusion.

Lyndon Johnson didn't figure things out in time. Although feeling against the war was growing stronger, and divisions in the country more intense, he believed that he could convince the nation to continue.

Johnson was getting advice from experts who said that the war was winnable, and that if we did not win it, Asia would "fall like a row of *dominoes*" to the Communists. Many Americans supported this stand, so he persisted in sending men and money to Vietnam and in making speeches to the people telling them why. The country grew further and further divided between those who supported the war as a crusade for freedom and those who felt it was immoral and a mistake. Each side bitterly questioned the patriotism of the other.

But Johnson had been elected in 1964 by the largest *landslide* ever up till then. He still felt that he could convince the people that he was right.

A man named Allard Lowenstein, though, thought differently. He believed in democracy and in changing things

Allard Lowenstein helped to convince people that working in elections was the best way to end the unpopular war in Vietnam. He traveled from college to college giving speeches to tell students that if they didn't like what was happening in their country, elections were the best way to help change things. (Time, Inc.)

Senator Eugene McCarthy campaigning in New Hampshire. Though he didn't win the 1968 New Hampshire Primary against President Lyndon Johnson, he did so much better than he was expected to do that it was regarded as a victory anyway. (Cynthia K. Samuels)

through the electoral process, so he began going around the country organizing something called the "Dump Johnson" *movement.* That was a group set up to try to convince someone—anyone—to run against Johnson in the elections that year and to prove, by getting a lot of people to vote against Johnson, that many people opposed the war.

He found a senator from Minnesota named Eugene J. McCarthy, who agreed to challenge Johnson for the Democratic nomination for president in 1968.

Troops of volunteers—mostly students—went to work for McCarthy, and they raised money through a group of antiwar businessmen and women. Though they didn't have any of the party organization or other usual tools at their disposal, they had an army of committed volunteers.

McCarthy did so well in the first election, the New Hampshire primary, that a more popular figure, Senator Robert Kennedy of New York, announced that he, too, would try to put Johnson out of office. In March of 1968, Johnson went on TV to give one of his many reports on the progress of the war. At the end, he said, "I shall not

Lyndon Johnson shocks America by announcing in a television address on March 30, 1968, that he will not run again for president. (Wide World Photos, Inc.)

seek and I will not accept the nomination of my party for another term as your president." America was stunned that a man of such power and energy would give up only four years after the biggest election victory in American history. Johnson's withdrawal led to chaos in the Democratic party, especially since Robert Kennedy, the new front-runner, was assassinated. McCarthy went on to the end of the campaign but lost the nomination to Johnson's vice president, a respected former senator named Hubert Humphrey, in a convention marred by violence and bitter demonstrations. But the war brought him down, too. Humphrey was defeated in the fall election by Republican Richard Nixon.

Lyndon Johnson had made a fatal mistake, one no elected person can afford: he had forgotten to pay attention to the political reality of governing. No one is too powerful to fall if he forgets to listen to the voters. And each voter, when he chooses to join with others who agree with him, has the power to elect or to bring down anyone—even the president of the United States.

Chapter 2
Who Runs and Why?

When there are big issues like war and peace, as there were in 1968, you can see that people may choose to run for office so that they can influence those issues. But people choose to run for office for lots of other reasons. Although the candidates are as varied as the jobs, there are several traditional types.

Most cities and towns have groups of people who get involved in government and elections early in their lives and keep on for a long time. They may help other people run, make sure there is enough money to run, or help in the many jobs that have to be done to win an election. But, after a while, some of these people get restless and want to get elected themselves. They have *paid their dues* as workers in the organization, and they've gained experience. Now *they* want a turn, so they often run for office themselves, and expect the same support they gave to others. Sometimes they are referred to as *pols* or *old pols*. The "pol" stands of course for politics or politician, and it is often meant as an insult, but it needn't be one. Many honorable and dedicated people spend their lives working in politics.

Then there are the women, blacks, and other groups who start in politics because they feel they are not being

David Lawrence, shown here posing with some kids in the mid-1940s, spent twenty years in government, first as mayor of Pittsburgh (1945-1959) and later as governor of Pennsylvania (1959-1963). Though he had enormous power in his state, he is remembered as a man who used his power well, to help rebuild a polluted and failing city into a great example of urban renewal. He was an "old pol" and a "political boss," but is an example of the way power can be used to accomplish good things. (Carnegie Library, Pittsburgh, PA)

treated fairly. They may decide to run for office to bring more progress to their group, whether that group is one seeking women's rights or civil rights.

In Cleveland, Ohio, two brothers did just that. In a city where blacks had been discriminated against, Carl and

Carl [L] and Louis [R] Stokes outside the United States Capitol. These two brothers from Cleveland helped show that black Americans can succeed in politics. Carl was the first black mayor of a major American city, and Louis serves as a leader in the United States House of Representatives. (Office of Rep. Louis Stokes)

Louis Stokes were determined that their race would not keep them down. They lived in a housing project in Cleveland, and their mother worked as a live-in maid and could only take care of them on weekends. They were so poor that Carl had to quit high school and go to work when he was seventeen.

He joined the army during World War II and finished high school after the war was over. Then he worked his way through college and law school. In 1967, after several years as a state representative, Carl became the first black mayor of a big American city. After two terms as mayor of Cleveland, he went on to work in television news, and later became a judge.

Carl's brother Louis began in politics by suing the state of Ohio. Louis claimed that the state had unfairly set things up so a black could never get elected, even in some black districts. He won the lawsuit and later ran for the United States House of Representatives, and won. Just as his brother had been the first black mayor, in 1968 Louis became the first black congressman from Ohio. He serves as a distinguished and highly respected member of the House of Representatives.

Fame

During World War II, one of the most popular people in the United States was the American general who led the Allies to victory in Europe. His name was Dwight David Eisenhower and he had never been in politics. But he had been a great hero during a long and difficult war, so he was extremely well liked. After the war, he became president of Columbia University, but both political parties, the Republicans and the Democrats, begged him to run for president.

They knew that he could get elected and that whichever party had "Ike" for a candidate would be in power, probably for two terms—or eight years. They were right, too. "I Like Ike" was the word for both 1952 and 1956, and since Eisenhower chose the Republicans, they were the party that *held the White House* all that time.

But Ike was by no means the only person to run for office on fame from another career. Senator Bill Bradley of New Jersey was a great basketball player for the New York Knicks. He was known for that all over the country, and although he was Princeton educated and honored for his schoolwork with a Rhodes Scholarship, one of the finest academic honors you can receive, the fame he got as a basketball player was a bigger help in getting him elected. His education meant that he would be a smart senator, but his days as "Dollar Bill Bradley" of the Knicks meant that when he ran, people already knew and liked him. The combination was perfect, and he won. In subsequent elections, of course, he had to run on his record as a senator. Once you're *in* office, the fame is replaced by responsibility.

Another senator who was elected because of his fame was unable to maintain the affection his state had felt for him. Jeremiah Denton of Alabama was a prisoner of war in North Vietnam for almost eight years. When he was released he went home to Alabama and began to build a political career. In 1980 he ran for the Senate from that state, and used, as was his right, his history as a war hero and patriot as a basis for his campaign. He won.

"Dollar Bill" Bradley in a dramatic moment during his years as a New York Knick. His career as a popular basketball star helped him become well-known, and that's a big help in politics. He was elected Senator from New Jersey in 1978, and reelected in 1984. (Wide World Photos, Inc.)

But when his term ended in 1986, the voters decided that, war hero or not, they didn't like his record in the Senate as well as they liked the potential of his opponent, and he was defeated for reelection. Fame can only take you so far if the voters decide you haven't been doing what they want.

Jeremiah Denton when he was a prisoner of war in Vietnam. While he was photographed, he blinked the word "torture" in Morse code with his eyes and got the word out that prisoners were being mistreated. He was elected a United States Senator from Alabama in 1980, but failed in a reelection bid in 1986. (Wide World Photos, Inc.)

Fame worked for Fred Grandy, who had played Gopher on the TV show "Love Boat," and was later elected to Congress, and for Senator John Kerry, who became famous as a Vietnam veteran who opposed the war in Vietnam after he came home. He ran once for the House of Representatives and lost, was elected lieutenant governor of Massachusetts and then won election to the Senate from that state in 1984.

Fame worked best of all, though, for a movie and television actor named Ronald Reagan. He served two terms as governor of California and was president of the United States for two terms beginning in 1981.

Good Neighbors

Though fame is a great political asset, leading a community fight against a big problem is just as good. Sometimes being involved in a community problem will get a person interested in changing the way things work. Maybe there is a dangerous corner and no one will put in a stop sign. Maybe local school assignments are unfairly made. You may get involved in your neighborhood over this one issue and go on to decide that you are able to bring about changes in other areas as well.

One person who found this was so was Harriet Woods, who served as *lieutenant governor* of Missouri. She got started in politics because of a manhole cover.

There were a lot of little kids in her neighborhood, but a loose manhole cover on the street in front of her house meant that every time a car drove by, the noise of the clunking cover woke up the kids from their naps. The

Harriet Woods greets some young constituents. She got started in politics because of a neighborhood problem and went on to build a state-wide career. (Shepard Sherbell, Picture Group)

noise was waking up her kids, too. No one seemed to care down at city hall, so Mrs. Woods decided to get involved. She persuaded the town to get the manhole fixed, and since it took a lot of political organizing to convince the city to do the repair, and she had learned how to get people working together for change, she decided to stay in politics. She went on to be elected to several jobs in the state including lieutenant governor.

Good Citizens

It sounds corny, but a lot of times people enter government because they want to do something good for their country. If you ever get a chance to talk to your senator or congressman, or mayor or sheriff, or anyone else who holds elective office, ask if he or she makes enough money. You will find that most of them could earn a lot more in a job in what is called the *private sector*. That's work done for nongovernment or private businesses. Jobs outside politics and government often pay a lot more to talented people.

But for many public officials the chance to make real changes in their country, to fight injustice, or to do things the way they think best is reason enough to enter government.

Two of the most famous of these people were also from two of the wealthiest families in our country. The first is Democrat John F. Kennedy, the thirty-fifth president of the United States, who was raised with public service as a main family value. Despite his wealth and the power his father had, Kennedy built experience as a politician through local Massachusetts organizations, became a congressman, then a senator, and finally, president of the United States.

It was he who told a hopeful nation in January of 1961, "Ask not what your country can do for you, ask what you can do for your country." Keeping with his family's

John Kennedy signs a campaign souvenir for a young admirer during the 1960 campaign. One of Kennedy's great wishes as president was to bring young people into government and convince them that serving their country was a great thing to do. (*The Plain Dealer*, Cleveland, OH)

tradition, his nephew Joe Kennedy, Jr., was elected in 1986 to the seat in the House of Representatives held years before by his Uncle Jack.

Even wealthier was Republican Nelson Rockefeller, who held many jobs in several Republican presidential administrations. He also served as governor of New York

Nelson Rockefeller greets young people in Watts, a Los Angeles ghetto. A leader of the Republican party, the wealthy Rockefeller spent his entire adult life in politics and government service. (Wide World Photos, Inc.)

State. Although he made several tries for the White House, he was never able to get his party's nomination. He did serve as vice president under Gerald Ford, though, and spent almost his entire adult life in one form of public service or another.

Power Trips

Sometimes people run for office because they want power. Since holding office gives you a lot of influence over what happens to your country—and to the people who live in it—that power can be attractive to people. That doesn't mean that they necessarily do a bad job, though, because even if they run for office only for the power, they know that if they don't please people they won't get elected again.

Of course, once in a while there are people who go into politics only to get rich. They use their jobs to increase their wealth—either by taking money that belongs to the government or by getting paid to do things they shouldn't do. But it doesn't happen all that often. And when it does, those who are caught are punished, and usually defeated if they try to run again.

That's the biggest difference in this system. No matter how much power you have, the voters always have more, because they have the power to take your powerful job away from you.

Chapter 3

Political Parties

As you have probably figured out, even the process of getting a nomination to run for office is complicated. Nobody just wakes up one morning as a candidate. No matter how good you are, you still have to be a part of the political system in order to be chosen as the one to represent your party in the elections. Here's how it works:

In this country, the first thing you have to do is to choose a party to belong to. A party is a group of people who work together to get their members elected. Most of the time people choose to join one of the two *major parties* in the United States, either the *Republicans* or the *Democrats*. Each party has its own set of ideas and list of positions on *issues*. That set of ideas and positions is called their *platform*. Even if a candidate doesn't agree with all of the positions his party may hold, it still helps to define his campaign if he takes on the party identity.

That identity comes with a slew of very practical services. Parties raise money and recruit volunteers to work in campaigns. They also have offices in most cities and states to which candidates can turn for help. These party offices have computer programs to do mailings, have experts to help you design your campaign strategy and to write

The 1976 Republican Convention cheers for nominee Gerald Ford. (Wide World Photos, Inc.)

and help produce television commercials, and provide all sorts of help. Look at chapters seven and eight and you'll see how much help you need!

Signing Up

That help begins right when you *register to vote*. It would really mess things up if any person who wanted to could vote as many times as she wished, so to keep track of voters, people are not allowed to vote on election day unless they are *registered*. Each state has its own rules for that, but basically you have to sign up and give your name and address sometime before election day. Then, when you go to vote, officials look you up on the list of *registered voters,* and unless you appear on the list, you can't vote. If a parent or voting-age friend is willing to take you, you might like to go along with him to the polls and see for yourself how election day works. It is the best way to prove to yourself that politics is just people, convinced, one by one, to vote for one candidate over another.

Sample of a voter registration card from Minnesota.

VOTER REGISTRATION CARD. Type or print in ink.

X Name _____ Last _____ First _____ Middle Initial

X Township or City of Legal Residence ____ Township / or City / County

X Complete Address of Legal Residence (include street or rural mail route address) ____ House Number and Street or Rural Route Number

Apt. No. or Rural Box No. _____ City _____ Zip

X Date of Birth ____ Month / Day / Year _____ Telephone No. _____

X Address of Your Last Registration or Check if NONE ☐ ____ House Number/Street Name or Route Box Number _____ Apt. No.

City or Township _____ County _____ State _____ Zip

Previous Name (If changed since last registration) _____

W _____ P _____
S.D. No. _____

OFFICE USE ONLY
Election Day Voter Registration Proof:
__ Driver's License
__ Minn. I.D. Card
__ Witness
__ Prior Registration
__ Ineffective Notice
__ Student I. D.
Number if Applicable
_____

CHECK INSTRUCTIONS TO DETERMINE WHETHER YOU ARE QUALIFIED TO REGISTER

I certify that I will be at least 18 years old on election day and that I am a citizen of the United States, reside at the address shown above and will have resided in Minnesota for 20 days immediately preceding election day, and that I am not under guardianship of the person, have not been found by a court to be legally incompetent to vote, and have not been convicted of a felony without having my civil rights restored. I understand that giving false information to procure a registration is a felony punishable by not more than 5 years imprisonment and a fine of not more than $10,000, or both.

____ Date / /

X _____ Legal Signature of Voter Also sign the blue card

Changing Parties

In some states, people indicate which party they belong to when they register to vote. For many years, most people took on the party identity of their family. If your parents were Republican, so were you. Now, though, people seem to be searching for new reasons to belong to parties, and some of the old allegiances are breaking up. People call this sort of breakup *realignment.*

The story you read about Lyndon Johnson may have helped to start that realignment, or at least have created a willingness to change. People who had been lifelong Democrats had to face up to the fact that Lyndon Johnson was a Democrat, so if they didn't like the Vietnam War they had to vote against their party. Others were so angry at the demonstrations and discord the war created in their country that they were ready to leave the party and seek order somewhere else.

Then, in the early seventies, while Richard Nixon was president, there was a break-in at the Democratic party headquarters in the Watergate Apartments in Washington. It turned out that supporters of Republican President Nixon were involved. They were trying to spy on the Democrats, to learn their campaign plans for the 1972 presidential election. Nixon's office tried to cover up the connection between his supporters and the break-in, but the scandal just seemed to keep growing.

As people learned more and more about the way the Republican presidential campaign had been run, investigations also revealed other unpleasant facts about the way Mr. Nixon's White House had operated. Things got so bad that President Nixon resigned. He was succeeded by his vice president, Gerald Ford.

The whole thing made it tough for many people to continue to believe in public officials. The feeling that you just couldn't trust anybody even had a name: people called it the *Watergate Syndrome* and, coming on the heels of the Vietnam War, it split many Republicans from *their* automatic party identification in the same way that opposition to the war or to the demonstrators had done to the Democrats.

By 1976 people wanted change, and although Nixon had, in 1972, won reelection by a historic landslide, his Watergate resignation made it easier for Democrat Jimmy Carter, who ran as a "non-Washington" candidate, to beat Nixon's replacement, Gerald Ford.

Once Carter won, though, he had real problems. Under his presidency, the United States entered a period of economic difficulty. Then, too, it was under Carter that a group of Americans was held hostage for more than a year in the United States Embassy in Iran. Though ever since World War II the United States has had more registered Democrats than Republicans, the crises the country faced under Democrat President Carter drove many to vote against the Democrats and *for* Republican Ronald Reagan in 1980. Reagan defeated Carter by a humiliating margin that year.

The voters really liked Reagan. Many former Democrats began to call themselves Republicans. No one is sure, though, whether they will decide to stay Republicans and to turn the Republican party, instead of the Democrats, into a majority.

Party Labels

There has always been a real difference between the two parties. Historically, Republicans have been called the "party of business" and the Democrats have been the labor union and civil rights supporters. But the last few years have seen a lot of those differences blur. One difference that remains, though, is the attitude toward government. You can almost always figure that a Democrat will support more government assistance in our lives, and a Republican will seek less.

In each party, you will find both *liberals* and *conservatives*. Though the words "liberal" and "conservative" can mean different things to different people, liberals in most cases tend to believe that the *federal government* should have an active role in helping to solve problems. They usually believe that each state has special needs that influence official decisions, and that a central government like the one in Washington is the best tool to guarantee protection to citizens in *every* state. A liberal might argue, for example, that you can't protect people from pollution with state laws, since polluted rivers and polluted air move from one state to another. Only a government with power over all states could do it, they would claim.

Conservatives, on the other hand, might say that the federal government should stay out of local issues, and that the states and cities should solve these problems themselves. They might argue that someone in Washington can't decide about pollution in Des Moines, that only people on the scene can decide the best way to solve the problem.

Conservatives and liberals also differ frequently on taxation and on foreign affairs. And a person can be considered conservative about foreign policy and liberal about economic or social policy, or the other way around. In these areas, the labels change meaning from generation to generation. Supporting higher taxes might be "liberal" in one period of history and "conservative" in another. But you can be sure that though there are conservative Democrats and liberal Republicans, you are more likely to find liberals in the Democratic party and conservatives in the Republican, and that certain parts of the country are more liberal, or more conservative, than others. Strategists usually figure that the South is very conservative, for example, and that the Northeast is among the most liberal areas of the United States.

Independent Thinkers

Remember too that although most people consider themselves either Republicans or Democrats, some people decide that neither party is for them. They are still allowed to register to vote, though, as is any citizen over eighteen. They just call themselves *independents,* which means they are "independent" of both parties. These days many more people choose to call themselves independents and to vote for a candidate solely because of his ideas, instead of choosing someone because of his party affiliation.

For example, independents are very often likely to vote for the candidate of one party for the senate and of another for governor. If they like the specific candidates, they'll ignore their party labels.

A few voters may even choose some *third party* that appeals to them. There are a lot of parties in different parts of the United States that serve smaller groups of people and use their name and place on the ballot to call attention to their ideas, even though it is difficult for third party candidates to win elections.

Sometimes third parties are even able to nominate presidential candidates. In 1948, for example, some southerners felt that allowing blacks and whites in the same schools was wrong and believed that the Democrats were too concerned with the civil rights of black Americans. They formed a third party called the *Dixiecrats,* since they were people from "Dixie"—the South.

In 1980 voters who were dissatisfied with both President Carter and Republican candidate Ronald Reagan managed to nominate John B. Anderson as a *third party candidate.*

In neither case did the candidates do very well, but each made his point. They probably also taught a lesson to the people in the party they had left. Candidates and voters don't turn to a third party if their original political allies are satisfactory. When rebels leave to form a third party, those left behind are reminded that they must pay more attention to party members who might feel that their ideas are being ignored.

Sometimes there are even third parties who would change the whole idea of the United States if they were elected. Communist and Socialist candidates seek great changes in our economic and political systems and would like to alter some of our basic rules. Even so, if the parties can get themselves on the ballot, they are free to run. Democratic politics can't work unless all ideas are freely argued and discussed—even ideas that question the value of our system. Only the voters can decide which parts of our system to keep and which to change, and they need to hear all ideas in order to make that choice.

Regionalism

Often, though, no matter what party people choose, party ideas differ from one part of the country to another. In a nation this big, where you live can determine a whole lot about how you think. So if you are from Arizona, at a time when there are plenty of jobs there, you might feel differently about unemployment assistance than you would if you came from Michigan at a time when local automobile assembly plants were closing. You will certainly feel differently about oil prices if you live in Texas, where citizens drill, sell, and make a lot of money from oil, than you will if you live in New Hampshire, which has to buy its energy from other states or countries.

In Texas, high oil prices mean high profits. In New Hampshire, though, those same high prices mean a much higher cost of living, just for heating a house through a cold New England winter. So on issues like these, members of the same party might have very different opinions.

Issues in which where you live determines what you think are called *regional issues*. Since our country is so large, each party will have members whose opinions differ on these regional issues. As you can see, their opinions will depend on what state they came from. But those different people can still belong to the same party, and they tend to vote together, as a party group, on big questions where those regional issues don't interfere.

		A ★ DEMOCRATIC	B 🦅 REPUBLICAN	C ꭍ CONSERVATIVE	D 🔔 LIBERAL
1	Electors for President and Vice-President of the United States **Vote once** Electores para Presidente y Vice-Presidente de los Estados Unidos **Vote solamente una vez**	For President *Para Presidente* **Walter F. Mondale** *and y* **Geraldine A. Ferraro** For Vice-President *Para Vice-Presidente* ★ DEMOCRATIC 1A ☐	For President *Para Presidente* **Ronald Reagan** *and y* **George Bush** For Vice-President *Para Vice-Presidente* 🦅 REPUBLICAN 1B ☐	For President *Para Presidente* **Ronald Reagan** *and y* **George Bush** For Vice-President *Para Vice-Presidente* ꭍ CONSERVATIVE 1C ☐	For Presid *Para Presid* **Walter F. Mondal** *and y* **Geraldine A. Ferrar** For Vice-Presid *Para Vice-Presiden* 🔔 LIBERAL 1D ☐
11	Representative in Congress Representante en Congreso **Vote for one—Vote por uno**	**James H. Scheuer** 11A ☐ ★ DEMOCRATIC	**Robert L. Brandofino** 11B ☐ 🦅 REPUBLICAN	**Robert L. Brandofino** 11C ☐ ꭍ CONSERVATIVE	**James H. Scheue** 11D ☐ 🔔 LIBERAL

8th Cong. District

A sample 1984 ballot from New York. Because so many New Yorkers are Hispanic, the ballot is also in Spanish, as you can see.

**OFFICIAL BALLOT FOR
THE GENERAL ELECTION**

City of New York, County of Queens

November 6, 1984

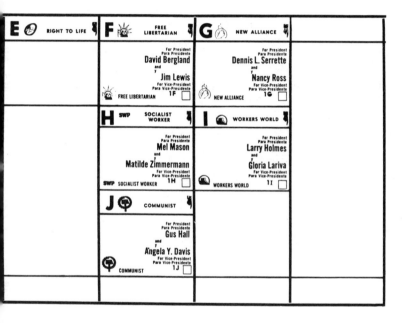

Candidates have to show an interest in regional issues. In America's farm belt, it is agriculture that draws candidates like 1984 presidential candidate Walter Mondale.

No matter where you live, though, you can't just pop into the board of elections and get your party's name on the ballot. In most states, this board, which governs the rules and fairness of elections in its area, requires a specific number of *signatures* before it will grant a candidate a place on the ballot. Lots of times you'll see people on the sidewalk, or outside the supermarket, asking people if they are registered voters and if they will sign a *petition* so that some candidate or new political party can appear on the ballot. If you get enough *valid signatures*—ones that can be checked out as those of eligible voters—then your party can appear on the ballot for the election.

One Person Who Did It
Tony Coelho,
Democrat of California,
who traded a lost dream for a new one

Tony Coelho, a Catholic farm boy from California, was always active in school politics. President of his high school student body, he also worked very hard at home, milking cows and doing other farm chores in the morning before

Tony Coelho [L] and his brother on their farm in California. They worked on the farm every day before and after school. (Office of Rep. Tony Coelho)

Representative Tony Coelho today. Disappointed that he couldn't become a priest, he went on to become a respected leader of the Democratic party. (Office of Rep. Tony Coelho)

school, and then again when school got out. During those tough school years, he was in an accident and hit his head. About a year later he began having seizures and blackouts. For years no one knew what was wrong, so he just went on as usual, working, studying, and being a leader among his classmates.

He had thought of being a lawyer, but while he was in college, his hero, President John Kennedy, was killed, and he decided to enter the Jesuit priesthood. His seizures continued, though, and finally he found a doctor who figured out what was the matter. He had epilepsy.

Though it is scary to think about blacking out or having "seizures," epilepsy is controllable with medication and it shouldn't have been a big deal. But the priesthood had ancient rules that said if you had epilepsy you weren't allowed to be a priest. Tony's dream was shattered.

Even his parents had trouble dealing with the disease. They were both the children of Portuguese immigrants, and in their old folk customs epilepsy meant possession by the devil. So his parents told him he wasn't sick, it was probably just his crazy fraternity life at college. He should just come home and calm down.

As you can imagine, he became very depressed, and moped around for a while. But then an old Jesuit friend got him a job working for the comedian Bob Hope, who was very kind to him and suggested that he try to forget his troubles by going into politics. Coelho went to work for California congressman B. F. Sisk and rose to the top of Sisk's staff. After thirteen years, Sisk retired and suggested Coelho run for the seat.

At first, his opponent tried to make Tony's epilepsy an issue in the race. The opponent told voters they shouldn't elect a guy who might have a fit while talking to the president. Coelho told the press, "People have fits at the White House all the time. At least I have an excuse."

He won, and went on to become not only a popular congressman and spokesman for his party, but Democratic Whip, the third highest office in the House of Representatives. He is also one of the most respected political tacticians in Congress. When he has any extra time, he spends it crusading to show people that epileptics can do anything, just as he did.

Chapter 4

A Winning Ticket

Once you decide what party to belong to, and you're sure that your party is represented on the ballot the voters will use on election day, you have an even harder job. You have to prove to your party that you are the one they should choose to run for office on their *ticket*. A ticket is a list of all the members of one party running for jobs in that particular election. For example, on the Republican ticket you might have a presidential candidate, a senator and congressman, a judge or two, and state legislators as well. In most states all candidates for office are listed on the ballot in columns, by party. Each party candidate can either help or hurt the others in the same column.

To be on the ticket, a candidate has to prove to the party not only that she is the best person for the job, but also that she can win the election. It doesn't matter if she would be good at the job if the party thinks no one will vote for her, because if nobody votes for her, she will never get a chance to prove how good she would have been.

Leader of the Pack

You've probably heard the expression "at the top of the ticket" or *"heading the ticket."* That means that your name

An excited 1976 Republican Convention cheers Ronald Reagan, who made his first try for the Republican nomination that year. He lost to President Gerald Ford, but was nominated and elected in 1980 and 1984. (Wide World Photos, Inc.)

is on top of the ballot for your party because you are running for the highest office in that particular election. If you are running for president, that's "heading the ticket." If there is no presidential election that year, it is usually the candidate for governor or senator who "heads the ticket."

If voters like the person at the head of the ticket, every candidate in that party is better off and gets more votes. Often, people even vote the *straight party ticket*. They just check off a blank at the top of the ballot or on the voting machine that reads "Democrat" or "Republican"—and that way they have voted for everyone in their party instead of deciding on the individual candidates.

When people choose members of different parties for different jobs, instead of voting the "straight ticket," they're *ticket splitting*. They might choose a Democrat for president, a Republican for senator and congressman and an Independent for judge.

Earlier in our history, political parties were so strong that their leaders could get you a job, get your kid out of jail if he got into trouble, or get you food or heating coal if you needed it—as long as you were a loyal party member. That's why, back then, the parties developed so much power. Later, your party had the power to see that your street got repaired, order a stop sign for your corner, or make sure that your garbage got collected. Loyal party neighborhoods got the best service. Now, of course, things have changed. Those benefits, if they come at all, tend to come from the government, not from the neighborhood political boss.

Even so, the old tradition of voting the straight party ticket, which goes back to the days of the old *bosses,* the leaders who got people coal and jobs and food, still exists. For example, in the South there is a funny expression, *yellow-dog Democrat*. People who are yellow-dog Democrats would vote for the Democratic candidate even if he were a "yellow dog"! That's how loyal they are to their party.

That tradition of party loyalty still has a strong hold in this country. That's why it's so important to have party support. (And it was why it was so hard to find someone willing to oppose Lyndon Johnson in 1967 and 1968!)

Besides, political parties have the money and skill to help you in your campaign. And local parties are connected to a national party, Republican or Democrat, which has organizational, computer, and TV skills and other benefits a local campaign would be hard-pressed to afford alone.

Of course, once in a while people can buck that system if they are creative and committed. Think back to Allard Lowenstein and the people who challenged Lyndon Johnson in 1968. They put themselves up against all that party power. Johnson probably thought it would be impossible for them to succeed when he had all the machinery!

One Person Who Did It
Barbara Mikulski,
Democrat of Maryland,
who won over her neighborhood, and then her state

Senator Barbara Mikulski isn't even five feet tall. And if you asked her she'd probably admit that she isn't exactly beautiful, either. But she has built a political career as steady and solid as any in our recent history.

A tiny, feisty woman with lots of energy and nerve, she makes you wonder at first how she convinced men to vote for her. She did it by being a skillful, old-fashioned politician.

Barbara grew up in Baltimore, where her parents owned a "mom and pop" grocery store. She worked there summers and after school. After college, she went on to become a social worker and worked with the unemployed, and with people on welfare, in her hometown. A graduate of mostly Catholic schools, she was influenced by the nuns in her schools and college and became interested in doing community work. When a planned superhighway would have meant demolishing a close-knit neighborhood, she organized the neighborhood and got the plans changed. A new political leader was born.

She was elected to the Baltimore City Council in 1971 and was so effective that she was chosen to help reform the rules for the national Democratic party. Then, in 1974, no well-known Democrat wanted to run against a popular Republican senator named "Mac" Mathias. Mikulski knew she probably couldn't win—no one would give money to

Senator Barbara Mikulski, who came from a blue-collar neighborhood in Baltimore. She used her work on neighborhood
issues to build a political base and was elected to the city council, then the House of Representatives, and, finally, the Senate.
(Office of Sen. Barbara Mikulski)

a campaign against a man so sure to be reelected. But she
ran anyway and got herself known in the state by doing
so. Then she returned to the city council, and when, in
1976, a House seat became vacant in Baltimore, she was
well known enough to win it. She served in the House
for ten years and eventually won Mathias's Senate seat in
1986, when he retired.

Chapter 5

Ways to Be Nominated

Okay. You have chosen a party and decided to run for office—to get your name on the ticket. There are three main ways of getting your party's nomination. All of them involve ways to convince your party that you are the one they should support. Before you do any of them, though, you have to *declare your candidacy*. In a formal ceremony or news conference, you announce that you want your party to choose you to be the person to run for a certain office. Once you've done that, you try to get the party to agree. With your method determined by the laws in your state, you go after the nomination.

If you are the only person who wants the nomination, then the chance to run is *uncontested*. That means there will be no contest to see who will get to run. But usually more than one person has his eye on a particular position. And for most offices, the most common way to become a candidate is to run for the right to run for office. Before any November election—state, local, or national—there are preelections called *primaries*. It was in a *primary election* in New Hampshire that Lyndon Johnson was humiliated by Eugene McCarthy and decided to call it quits.

Primaries may be held any time before the November general election day, which is the same all over the country.

When two or more people from the same party want to run for the same job, they run against each other in the primary and the winner gets to run in the general election. Any registered voter may vote in the primaries.

When voters get to the polls they ask for the ballot of one party or the other. If they live in a state where they had to register by party, they are automatically given the ballot for the party they chose when they registered.

Presidential Nominations

For the presidential nomination, the primaries are critical. Because there are so many primaries, candidates must organize early to have a staff working in each state where primaries take place. It's like running a whole series of presidential elections, though there are often more than two candidates per race. In the beginning of the *primary season* anyone with a dream of becoming president—if he can raise the money—tries to get organized and run.

The primary schedule begins in the winter of the election year, usually in New Hampshire, which traditionally holds the first presidential primary. States choose their primary election dates individually. Many states, especially those in the South, have decided to hold their primaries on the same day in March. Because there is so much at stake on that day, it is called *Super Tuesday*. The season continues, state by state, into the early summer. Each election day brings several more primaries.

Remember now, in each state there is a little campaign running. There are campaign managers and television commercials and staff. The campaign must have enough money

the 1980 Democratic Convention in
ticking up in the air tell each state dele-
ch state also has a telephone attached to
an call other delegations or candidate
ut what is going on. (Wide World

the old days, when there were few
cians had a lot of power to move del
date to another. But since the delega
y primary or caucus votes, the suspe
d of primary season, unless the con
ncommitted superdelegates can sv
e other.

to pay for these staffs and a strategy that will keep the campaign alive in so many different places. It also must keep the candidate visible without exhausting him in repeated campaign trips before the presidential race has officially begun.

Primaries are the most common way for parties in each state to decide which candidate to support.

Many states, though, have more complicated systems. In some states, you have to go to local *caucuses*. These are meetings of small groups of party members; any registered voters in that party may go. At a caucus, each party member who shows up at the meeting gets one vote. In some states, he votes for the person he thinks should be the candidate.

In others, he may vote for a *delegate* to a county or state *convention,* which will meet to choose a candidate. The voter will know that the person he sends to the convention will vote for his candidate. Lots of times, caucuses to elect nominees or the delegates to state conventions meet on the same night all over the state.

The first caucus is usually held in Iowa very early in February of the election year. The results of the Iowa meetings are one of the first indications of who might win the presidential nominations. That's why you see so many news reports about those "Iowa caucuses."

When a caucus does meet only to elect delegates to a convention, those delegates go to the convention committed to vote for the person they represent. But delegates are allowed to change their votes if no one wins on the *first ballot* or round of voting. The rules usually say that a person is free to vote for someone else if the convention keeps coming back with tie votes, or when no one candidate

Campaign workers count the votes at a state nominating convention. (© 1982 Richard Sobol)

wins the votes of a majority of the delegates. That's called a *deadlock*.

Other times, the candidate may *release* the delegates. If he knows he's never going to win, he may trade his delegates to someone else: "I'll let my people vote for you, and you promise to act the way I would have acted on trade, or education, or promise to give an important position in government to my campaign manager, or to me."

But
prim
a *na*
of th
or p
Puer
week

tion
had
in ea

date
cand
Each
on t
state
muc
to th

gate
from
in t
thos
go t
offic
are s

as h

A speaker's-eye view a
New York. The signs
gation where to sit. E
the sign poll, so they
headquarters to find
Photos, Inc.)

from every state. In
primaries, state polit
gates from one candi
are now determined
is often over by the e
is so close that those
things one way or t

There is another way to hold on to some of the tension, too. Occasionally, a state will vote in the primary to send its governor, or another state official, as a *favorite son*. They will name him or her as their nominee for president, even though they know they can't win. That way they hold out until they get to the convention and don't pledge their votes in advance. They can use these votes to negotiate with the nominee for promises about cabinet appointments or funding for their state.

Besides, you're never sure about the nominee until the first vote is taken on the convention floor. The first vote, which is usually on an issue or a rule of the convention, is sort of a test. Delegates will decide how to vote on rules or issues by looking at the position of the candidate they support. If their candidate is *for* something, they vote yes. If he is against it, they vote no. The position that wins helps to reveal who will be the winning candidate.

Standing for Something

Frequently, those crucial votes will be about the platform, or list of ideas, upon which the party will campaign. Sometimes there is enormous conflict over these ideas as the platform is being written. Before it is submitted to the convention, the platform is hammered out in a series of *hearings*. That's where interested people from all over the country may come to testify to the *platform committee* in an effort to make their favorite issue a part of the campaign. Civil rights groups, farmers, health and education interests, and many others make every effort to see that their point of view is part of the platform.

Of course, an elected president does not have to follow his party's platform; it isn't law. But it is the symbolic base of ideas that his party has chosen to support—as it supports him—and if he isn't comfortable with the ideas in the platform, he's going to have problems.

If you ran for class president on a platform that promised to get a smoking area in your school, your supporters would expect you to work with the principal to do just that. But if you believe that smoking is so unhealthy that it ought to be illegal in school, you're not going to be very comfortable pushing for a place for people to smoke. No candidate should run on a platform that feels wrong.

Since candidates want to feel right about the platform they must run on, debates can get pretty fierce. Once everyone has testified and the platform committee has completed its work and agreed on a document, that document is presented to the whole convention: The whole convention has to pass it. Supporters of every candidate must agree on the same set of ideas. Since those people were all supporting different candidates because they didn't agree to begin with, getting that support can be difficult.

Sometimes there are *floor fights*—battles on the convention floor—over which *planks*—or positions on issues, will be included. Since the winning candidate wants the convention to look unified and determined to elect him, he doesn't want a lot of fighting over individual issues. Sometimes candidates who are going to lose the nomination can still push their ideas into the platform by threatening a floor fight that would make the winner of the nomination look bad, or create hard feelings that would make supporters of a loser less likely to work in the election campaign.

New Jersey Democratic delegates celebrate because it was *their* state, in the roll call, that put Walter Mondale "over the top" and ensured that he had enough delegate votes to be nominated as 1984 Democratic candidate for president. (Wide World Photos, Inc.)

If two candidates are close in the number of delegates they have, suspense builds. The candidates can maneuver with each other over issues until one or the other gets the majority of votes and is declared the winner.

Conventions Matter

Even without suspense, though, the conventions are very important. If a candidate is to launch his campaign well, he must have the national party behind him. The national convention is like a gigantic pep rally and is a great way to get people involved in the election. It is also an opportunity for powerful politicians from all over the country to meet and work out ways to help candidates running for office in their states.

Then, too, since the conventions are televised, they also provide the national exposure that politicians require and love. When a party wants to make a point, the free national television time provided by a convention is incredibly valuable.

Making It Official

Once the platform is passed, the nominee is officially selected by a *roll call* of the state delegations. The state's name is called and the party chairperson of that state casts the votes allotted to his state. You may have seen film of these voting roll calls in documentaries. "Mr. Chairman," says the state chair, "the great state of ———— casts [however many votes that state is permitted] for [whomever the state chose in its primary or caucus]."

After each state has cast its votes, as they were dealt out in the primaries and caucuses, or struggled through a number of roll-call votes to reach a majority for one candidate, one supporter of the winner will probably rise and move that the candidate be nominated by *acclamation*. This means that the whole convention agrees to the nomination of the winner and that all other votes are wiped out, to make the nomination *unanimous*. Usually, since the party wants to win in the fall, this effort at harmony is accepted, and the candidate is nominated by acclamation.

Chapter 5

Ways to Be Nominated

Okay. You have chosen a party and decided to run for office—to get your name on the ticket. There are three main ways of getting your party's nomination. All of them involve ways to convince your party that you are the one they should support. Before you do any of them, though, you have to *declare your candidacy*. In a formal ceremony or news conference, you announce that you want your party to choose you to be the person to run for a certain office. Once you've done that, you try to get the party to agree. With your method determined by the laws in your state, you go after the nomination.

If you are the only person who wants the nomination, then the chance to run is *uncontested*. That means there will be no contest to see who will get to run. But usually more than one person has his eye on a particular position. And for most offices, the most common way to become a candidate is to run for the right to run for office. Before any November election—state, local, or national—there are preelections called *primaries*. It was in a *primary election* in New Hampshire that Lyndon Johnson was humiliated by Eugene McCarthy and decided to call it quits.

Primaries may be held any time before the November general election day, which is the same all over the country.

When two or more people from the same party want to run for the same job, they run against each other in the primary and the winner gets to run in the general election. Any registered voter may vote in the primaries.

When voters get to the polls they ask for the ballot of one party or the other. If they live in a state where they had to register by party, they are automatically given the ballot for the party they chose when they registered.

Presidential Nominations

For the presidential nomination, the primaries are critical. Because there are so many primaries, candidates must organize early to have a staff working in each state where primaries take place. It's like running a whole series of presidential elections, though there are often more than two candidates per race. In the beginning of the *primary season* anyone with a dream of becoming president—if he can raise the money—tries to get organized and run.

The primary schedule begins in the winter of the election year, usually in New Hampshire, which traditionally holds the first presidential primary. States choose their primary election dates individually. Many states, especially those in the South, have decided to hold their primaries on the same day in March. Because there is so much at stake on that day, it is called *Super Tuesday*. The season continues, state by state, into the early summer. Each election day brings several more primaries.

Remember now, in each state there is a little campaign running. There are campaign managers and television commercials and staff. The campaign must have enough money to pay for these staffs and a strategy that will keep the campaign alive in so many different places. It also must keep the candidate visible without exhausting him in repeated campaign trips before the presidential race has officially begun.

Primaries are the most common way for parties in each state to decide which candidate to support.

Many states, though, have more complicated systems. In some states, you have to go to local *caucuses*. These are meetings of small groups of party members; any registered voters in that party may go. At a caucus, each party member who shows up at the meeting gets one vote. In some states, he votes for the person he thinks should be the candidate.

In others, he may vote for a *delegate* to a county or state *convention,* which will meet to choose a candidate. The voter will know that the person he sends to the convention will vote for his candidate. Lots of times, caucuses to elect nominees or the delegates to state conventions meet on the same night all over the state.

The first caucus is usually held in Iowa very early in February of the election year. The results of the Iowa meetings are one of the first indications of who might win the presidential nominations. That's why you see so many news reports about those "Iowa caucuses."

When a caucus does meet only to elect delegates to a convention, those delegates go to the convention committed to vote for the person they represent. But delegates are allowed to change their votes if no one wins on the *first ballot* or round of voting. The rules usually say that a person is free to vote for someone else if the convention keeps coming back with tie votes, or when no one candidate

Campaign workers count the votes at a state nominating convention. (© 1982 Richard Sobol)

wins the votes of a majority of the delegates. That's called a *deadlock*.

Other times, the candidate may *release* the delegates. If he knows he's never going to win, he may trade his delegates to someone else: "I'll let my people vote for you, and you promise to act the way I would have acted on trade, or education, or promise to give an important position in government to my campaign manager, or to me."

Presidential Conventions

But whether states ask voters to show their preferences in primaries, conventions, or caucuses, each party still holds a *national presidential nominating convention*. In the summer of the presidential election year, *delegates* selected by vote or party meeting, from the fifty states, plus territories like Puerto Rico, Guam, and the Virgin Islands, meet for a week. Usually one party meets in July, the other in August.

In some years, the nomination is all sewn up by convention time. Since there are so many primaries, voters have had a good chance to express their preferences. The winners in each state primary are assigned *convention delegates*.

Each *state delegation* is made up of supporters of candidates who did well in that state's primary or caucus. The candidate who got the most votes gets the most delegates. Each candidate gets a *proportion* of delegates depending on the percentage of the vote he or she received. Every state has its own formula. Each of these delegates is pretty much committed to a single candidate by the time he gets to the convention city.

The Democratic party also appoints some of its delegates automatically. They are elected officials and leaders from each state. Since party rules guarantee them positions in the state delegation, and they don't have to fight for those positions, they are called *superdelegates,* and usually go to the convention *uncommitted* to any candidate, at least officially. Around fifteen percent of the convention delegates are superdelegates.

It used to be that conventions were full of suspense, as hopefuls fought to capture the vote of every delegate

A speaker's-eye view at the 1980 Democratic Convention in New York. The signs sticking up in the air tell each state delegation where to sit. Each state also has a telephone attached to the sign poll, so they can call other delegations or candidate headquarters to find out what is going on. (Wide World Photos, Inc.)

from every state. In the old days, when there were fewer primaries, state politicians had a lot of power to move delegates from one candidate to another. But since the delegates are now determined by primary or caucus votes, the suspense is often over by the end of primary season, unless the contest is so close that those uncommitted superdelegates can swing things one way or the other.

There is another way to hold on to some of the tension, too. Occasionally, a state will vote in the primary to send its governor, or another state official, as a *favorite son*. They will name him or her as their nominee for president, even though they know they can't win. That way they hold out until they get to the convention and don't pledge their votes in advance. They can use these votes to negotiate with the nominee for promises about cabinet appointments or funding for their state.

Besides, you're never sure about the nominee until the first vote is taken on the convention floor. The first vote, which is usually on an issue or a rule of the convention, is sort of a test. Delegates will decide how to vote on rules or issues by looking at the position of the candidate they support. If their candidate is *for* something, they vote yes. If he is against it, they vote no. The position that wins helps to reveal who will be the winning candidate.

Standing for Something

Frequently, those crucial votes will be about the platform, or list of ideas, upon which the party will campaign. Sometimes there is enormous conflict over these ideas as the platform is being written. Before it is submitted to the convention, the platform is hammered out in a series of *hearings*. That's where interested people from all over the country may come to testify to the *platform committee* in an effort to make their favorite issue a part of the campaign. Civil rights groups, farmers, health and education interests, and many others make every effort to see that their point of view is part of the platform.

Of course, an elected president does not have to follow his party's platform; it isn't law. But it is the symbolic base of ideas that his party has chosen to support—as it supports him—and if he isn't comfortable with the ideas in the platform, he's going to have problems.

If you ran for class president on a platform that promised to get a smoking area in your school, your supporters would expect you to work with the principal to do just that. But if you believe that smoking is so unhealthy that it ought to be illegal in school, you're not going to be very comfortable pushing for a place for people to smoke. No candidate should run on a platform that feels wrong.

Since candidates want to feel right about the platform they must run on, debates can get pretty fierce. Once everyone has testified and the platform committee has completed its work and agreed on a document, that document is presented to the whole convention: The whole convention has to pass it. Supporters of every candidate must agree on the same set of ideas. Since those people were all supporting different candidates because they didn't agree to begin with, getting that support can be difficult.

Sometimes there are *floor fights*—battles on the convention floor—over which *planks*—or positions on issues, will be included. Since the winning candidate wants the convention to look unified and determined to elect him, he doesn't want a lot of fighting over individual issues. Sometimes candidates who are going to lose the nomination can still push their ideas into the platform by threatening a floor fight that would make the winner of the nomination look bad, or create hard feelings that would make supporters of a loser less likely to work in the election campaign.

New Jersey Democratic delegates celebrate because it was *their* state, in the roll call, that put Walter Mondale "over the top" and ensured that he had enough delegate votes to be nominated as 1984 Democratic candidate for president. (Wide World Photos, Inc.)

If two candidates are close in the number of delegates they have, suspense builds. The candidates can maneuver with each other over issues until one or the other gets the majority of votes and is declared the winner.

Conventions Matter

Even without suspense, though, the conventions are very important. If a candidate is to launch his campaign well, he must have the national party behind him. The national convention is like a gigantic pep rally and is a great way to get people involved in the election. It is also an opportunity for powerful politicians from all over the country to meet and work out ways to help candidates running for office in their states.

Then, too, since the conventions are televised, they also provide the national exposure that politicians require and love. When a party wants to make a point, the free national television time provided by a convention is incredibly valuable.

Making It Official

Once the platform is passed, the nominee is officially selected by a *roll call* of the state delegations. The state's name is called and the party chairperson of that state casts the votes allotted to his state. You may have seen film of these voting roll calls in documentaries. "Mr. Chairman," says the state chair, "the great state of ——— casts [however many votes that state is permitted] for [whomever the state chose in its primary or caucus]."

After each state has cast its votes, as they were dealt out in the primaries and caucuses, or struggled through a number of roll-call votes to reach a majority for one candidate, one supporter of the winner will probably rise and move that the candidate be nominated by *acclamation*. This means that the whole convention agrees to the nomination of the winner and that all other votes are wiped out, to make the nomination *unanimous*. Usually, since the party wants to win in the fall, this effort at harmony is accepted, and the candidate is nominated by acclamation.

Choosing a Vice President

Now it is time for the nominee to choose a vice-presidential candidate. It is the right of the nominee to select who will run with him. Usually that choice is made not only on whether the candidate will be good at the job, but with political considerations in mind.

If the presidential candidate is from the Northeast, the vice-presidential one will likely be from the South or Far West. That way more regions of the country will be interested in the ticket. If the presidential nominee is extremely conservative, the vice-presidential one may be less so, to insure the support of both parts of the party. The nominee tries to *balance the ticket*.

Ronald Reagan was far more conservative than George Bush, who ran against him in the primaries in 1980, but he chose Bush anyway, to unite the diverse ideas in the party and to create a "unifying" ticket. Reagan also took on an important staff member from the Bush campaign, James Baker, as a top advisor to his campaign and as top White House aide after he was elected. By hiring a Bush person he further unified the two *factions* of his party and was free to concentrate on beating the Democrats instead of having to worry about keeping peace in his own party.

It is said that John Kennedy picked Lyndon Johnson in 1960 not only because Kennedy was from Massachusetts and Johnson was from Texas, but also because Johnson had been such a powerful leader in the Senate. Kennedy decided he would rather have Johnson as vice president, on his side, than in the Senate, where Johnson could have been an effective rival.

No matter why he or she is chosen, the vice-presidential candidate must also be confirmed by the convention. After that vote, each nominee comes to the convention hall and speaks. The vice-presidential candidate speaks earlier, so the presidential candidate can have the final word.

On the last night of the convention, the presidential nominee gives a speech that is designed to inspire everyone. Then he brings out the vice-presidential nominee. All the party leaders join them on the podium and there is cheering and music and general craziness, much like a rally before an athletic event. If the evening has been well-coordinated, everyone goes home ready to work hard for the ticket and to see that their party wins in the fall.

One Person Who Did It

Margaret Chase Smith,
*Republican of Maine,
who was a true pioneer*

Margaret Chase Smith first came to Washington on a class trip in 1916. To get there she borrowed sixty dollars from her grandfather and he made her sign a note for it and pay interest. But she saw the city and got to shake hands with President Woodrow Wilson, and she knew she'd come back.

She did, in 1937, with her congressman husband, Clyde. But he died after only three years, and she was appointed to take his place in Congress. She served in the House, and then the Senate, for the next thirty-two years. The first time she ran for the Senate, her opponent used the slogan "The Senate Is No Place for a Woman." She never answered those sorts of comments and has said that she did best by ignoring them.

The first woman to be elected to both the House and the Senate, she had a long and very distinguished career. She told reporters that women today would do better in politics if they would help one another. To her, women are too quick to compete with one another instead.

Although military defense was her issue for much of her career, she is perhaps most famous for using her political influence in a brave and dangerous way. During her Senate term, there was a senator from Wisconsin named Joseph McCarthy who claimed that there were many Communists in the United States government. To this day there is argument about whether he was right, but correct or not, his tactics were a problem for many people.

Senator Margaret Chase Smith in 1950, the year she gave her famous speech about Senator Joe McCarthy. She almost always wore a rose—it was her trademark. On the day Senator Robert Kennedy was assassinated in California in 1968, she took off her rose and left it on his Senate desk as a tribute. (Margaret Chase Smith Library Center, Skowhegan, ME)

What he would do was accuse people of being Communists or of having friends who were. Soon government officials and many other Americans were afraid to be seen with anyone who might be accused of being a Communist, because once McCarthy accused you, it was very hard to convince people he was wrong.

Even the Congress was scared. Mrs. Smith decided that it was time for someone to speak up. She rose on the floor of the Senate in June of 1950 and said, "I speak as a Republican. I speak as a woman. I speak as a United States senator. I speak as an American. I don't want to see the Republican party ride to political victory on the four horsemen of calumny—fear, ignorance, bigotry, and smear." It was an old-fashioned phrase, but it did the trick.

"I took about all I could from his kind," she told the *Washington Post* many years later. "We were living by fear. Nobody knows what it was like. You could hardly go down to the Senate dining room with someone for fear that man [McCarthy] would get on the floor and denounce you as the newest Communist in the government. . . . He was a ruthless, ruthless man. I like to think my speech was the first step on the road to his eventual censure."

Senator Smith took a political risk: she believed she was right and was willing to risk being labeled a Communist by McCarthy and perhaps being denied reelection, to take the position she believed in. That sort of political leadership, from the first woman elected to both houses of Congress and the first woman to be nominated for president at a political convention, was her most memorable act. It also made it easier for others to follow, because she had taken the huge chance of going first—something politicians are sometimes afraid to do.

Just as Tony Coelho had the courage to rebuild his life when epilepsy stopped his dream, Mrs. Smith had the courage to take an unpopular stand that, she believed, would help to save her country.

Chapter 6
Different Elections

Remember that there is more than one kind of election. The ones you know the most about are called *general elections*. Those are the ones that elect public officials. But there is more than one kind of general election, though most are held the first Tuesday after the first Monday in November of even-numbered years.

The Constitution was written to give power both to the United States, or federal government, and to the individual *state governments*. The Founding Fathers were very careful to leave plenty of power for the states. They also designated several jobs in the federal government to which people were elected from each individual state. Complicated? Not really.

Presidential Elections

There is, first of all, a presidential election. Every four years, in years divisible by four (like 1948, 1960, 1984), we elect the president of the United States. Every registered voter in the United States may vote for the president.

You probably know that when people vote for president, they are actually voting for *electors,* or members of

the *electoral college*. The electoral college isn't a school, it is a group of people sent to cast the votes of their state for president. When the country started, those who wrote the Constitution were nervous about the way things might turn out. So instead of letting the president be elected directly by the voters, they set up another system.

Each state would hold an election, and the winner in each state would be named by that state's representatives at a meeting called the electoral college. If one candidate gets fifty-one percent in a state, and another gets forty-nine percent, the winner still gets all the votes for that state. The system is *winner-take-all*. Though some people would rather see the United States move toward *direct election* of presidents, we still elect our chief executives by sending representatives to the electoral college to cast the votes reflecting what happened in their states.

Federal Elections

But there are other *federal offices*. The Congress, made up of 100 senators and 435 representatives, runs the federal government in partnership with the president and the Supreme Court. But the two senators per state, and the representatives from each state, are elected only by voters registered in the state they represent.

A Senate term is six years. The terms are arranged so that every two years, one third of our one hundred senators must run for reelection.

A House term is two years. Therefore, all 435 members of the House of Representatives must run every two years. And because their jobs are only good for two years, they

REPUBLICANS FOR A STRONGER RIVER VALE

WALTER JONES
for MAYOR

PAT GEIER
for COUNCIL

BERNIE SALMON
for COUNCIL

VOTE REPUBLICAN
NOVEMBER 4

If you need a ride to the polls, please call:
391-4973 / 666-3011 / 664-3814

REPUBLICANS FOR A STRONGER RIVER VALE
39 Leona Court, River Vale, NJ 07675

**YOU BE
THE JUDGE**

"KEEP RIVER VALE
A GOOD PLACE
IN WHICH TO LIVE"

River Vale's

Best Qualified

Candidate

for

Township

Council

IS THERE A DIFFERENCE BETWEEN OUR CANDIDATES FOR MAYOR AND COUNCIL AND THEIRS? YOU BE THE JUDGE

OUR CANDIDATES

FINANCES — In just 2 years a surplus of $300,000 while paying off $165,000 in debts — a stabilizing effect on taxes.

YOUTH CENTER — Appointed a committee of youth group leaders to help determine use and costs involved.

COUNCIL EFFECTIVENESS — Put forth 332 of the 350 issues voted on.

ROADS — Repaving now underway on a pay-as-you-go basis.

CULVERT AND ROAD IMPROVEMENTS — on Poplar Road at no additional cost to River Vale taxpayers.

NEW PHONE SYSTEM — Now installed in Town Hall — provides better service and saves $10,000 a year.

INSURANCE COSTS — Held down by joining a self-insurance pool with other towns.

BIPARTISAN INVOLVEMENT — Citizens appointed to committees for roads, computers, and youth center.

RECREATION — New bleachers, fencing and lights installed.

SENIOR CITIZENS — Approved funds for center expansion, senior programs and walkway improvements.

THE OPPOSITION

FINANCES — In 8 out of the last 10 years, depleted the surplus in every election year, resulting in higher taxes the following year.

YOUTH CENTER — Trying to use it for political advantage. Want to put up the building without knowing what it costs to insure, heat, furnish and maintain. Who will be responsible for supervision?

COUNCIL EFFECTIVENESS — Introduced only 18 of the 350 issues for vote.

ROADS — 13 years of pot holes and decay.

Thank You from Walter, Pat and Bernie
for the consideration you have given us as candidates for Mayor and Council in the coming election. It has been a privilege to serve you in the offices we now hold, and we hope you will find our performance worthy of future support on November 4.

REPUBLICANS FOR A STRONGER RIVER VALE

Paid for by M. Smith, Treas., 39 Leona Court, River Vale, NJ must always be watching to see how to run their next election. That's a really tough political job! Only voters from their *congressional district* may vote for a House candidate. The U.S. Constitution combines with individual state laws to determine who votes in which elections. You can vote for your senator if you are a registered voter in his state, but if you're from New York and you admire the senator from Kansas, you can't vote for her. And you only vote for the congressman, or representative, who is from your *district,* the area near your home assigned to that congressman.

Elections held in the intervals between presidential election years are called *off-year* elections. Fewer people bother to vote when there is no presidential election excitement to get them to the polls. Even so, two-thirds of the senators and all of the congressmen must run in off-years.

State Races

There are *state-wide races* that are also general elections. The governor of your state runs for office in the whole state. In a couple of states the governor runs every two years, in most states four. The entire state gets to vote for the governor, the lieutenant-governor, if there is one, and often for other jobs too, like attorney general.

But what about your state legislature, that "state congress" that passes the local laws the Constitution was so careful to provide for? The states and the federal government have different duties. Somebody has to write and pass those state and local laws, and so each state has its own *state legislature.*

These state legislators are almost always elected on the same election days as the national and state candidates; each one is elected only by the voters in his or her district. Usually a district for a state legislator is a neighborhood or another smaller area.

State legislatures design both the congressional and state legislative districts. When Democrats control the state legislatures, they try to map out these districts to make it easier for Democrats to get elected. When Republicans control the state legislatures, they try to make it easier for Republican candidates. If they try too hard, and make the districts too complicated just so their party will have the advantage, that's called *gerrymandering*.

Local Elections

If you've been paying attention you have noticed that a whole area of government is missing from this list. Where are the mayors, the county commissioners, the school board members—all the other people who make your life go on day by day? Well, they do run for office too, but sometimes they run on a different election day. Often, because they run in *local elections,* people don't pay enough attention to the candidates or even come out and vote. That means that sometimes people are elected to do those local jobs by a very small number of voters, even though what those officials decide will affect everybody.

You might want to ask your parents if they vote in local elections, because the policies in your school district, or the bike or skateboard or curfew rules in your town, are decided by the people who win those local races.

One Person Who Did It

Mike Mansfield,
Democrat of Montana,
Ambassador to Japan

Mike Mansfield ran away to join the navy when he was fifteen years old. His father worked as a hotel porter in New York, and his mom died when he was young. Because his father was unable to take care of him, he was sent to live with an aunt and uncle in Great Falls, Montana. He worked in their grocery store, but soon started running away, hopping freight trains and getting pretty far before he got caught and sent home.

Just before he turned fifteen, Mike enlisted in the navy. He lied about his age and got away with it. He made seven trips back and forth across the Atlantic at the beginning of World War I before somebody figured out that they were sailing with a kid in their ranks.

When he was finally found out, the navy sent him home to Montana. Undaunted, he joined the army. When he was old enough, he was sent to Siberia, China, and the Philippines for his military service, and he fell in love with Asia.

When he got out of the army he went to work in the copper mines of Butte, Montana, as a shoveler. At twenty-four he went back to school, at the Montana School of Mines, as a special student. When he met the woman who would become his wife, she convinced him to finish his schooling, not just as a special student, but in search of a degree. He ended up a professor of Far Eastern history.

In 1942 he was elected to replace the retiring Jeannette

Rankin, the first woman ever to have served in the House of Representatives. His knowledge of Asia so impressed President Franklin Roosevelt that he sent Mansfield to China on a confidential mission in 1944, during World War II.

After ten years in the House, Mansfield was elected to the Senate. He served there through the presidencies of Eisenhower, Kennedy, Johnson, Nixon, and Ford, most

Mike Mansfield, football hero. This picture is from the Montana School of Mines yearbook for 1928. A miner in Montana, Mansfield started at the school as a special student but went on to become a professor before he ran for the House and the Senate. (Montana School of Mines, Butte, MT, and T.J. Reget)

of that time as majority leader. The majority leader sets the schedule for votes and the order in which proposed laws and presidential nominations will be considered by the Senate. He also speaks for all the Senate members of the *majority party*. It was Mansfield who replaced Lyndon Johnson as Senate leader when Johnson became vice president, and he remained in that post through the Kennedy

Ambassador Mike Mansfield in his Tokyo office. He has been one of the most successful of our ambassadors to Japan. It is a big job because Japan is a major ally and trading partner of the United States, so the relationship between the two countries has to be protected. (Office of the Ambassador)

assassination, the Vietnam War, and the trauma of Watergate.

Throughout it all, as he addressed the nation after Kennedy died, as he led the Senate in opposition to the war in Vietnam, as he helped to lead the country in those hard days and in the Watergate days that followed, Mike Mansfield was revered as a man of honor and integrity, humor and leadership.

When he announced his retirement from the Senate in 1976 by saying that he and his wife Maureen wanted a bit of rest, President Carter named him ambassador to Japan. That gave him a chance to go back to the Asia he so loved. And though Ronald Reagan didn't agree with Jimmy Carter about much, he agreed with that decision. When he was elected in 1980, Reagan kept Mansfield in the job, and in 1986 Mansfield became the longest-serving ambassador to Japan.

Anytime you think you can't be a good guy and succeed in politics, think again. Mike Mansfield of Montana succeeded, and remained among the most respected men in public life.

Chapter 7
Getting Organized

One thing is always true in politics: no matter how big the election, whether you are running for president or dogcatcher, you still have to have a good campaign if you want to win. And that campaign must be built in several areas. You wouldn't want a baseball team of great hitters who couldn't field, and you wouldn't want a doctor who could figure out what was wrong with you but didn't know how to treat it. Same with politics—you have to run your campaign so that it works well in every area.

Of course, we know you need a *message*. It would be really unfair to voters to run for office just because you wanted the job, if you had no ideas about how to improve things after you were elected.

You may have heard about 1984, during the Democratic race for the presidential nomination, when Vice President Walter Mondale was running against Senator Gary Hart. Mr. Mondale felt that Gary Hart didn't have much to say except that he was "new" and had "new" ideas. Mondale kept saying that Hart claimed he had new ideas but never told anyone what they were. He wanted to show that he believed Hart didn't have much to offer except talk.

At the time, there was a funny hamburger commercial running on TV. A little old lady would walk up to the fast-food counter and say "Where's the beef?" and point to what looked like an empty hamburger bun. The commercial was for a fast-food place that claimed their hamburgers were bigger and better, so the old lady saying "Where's the beef?" was supposed to make the point that the competition had tiny, unimpressive hamburgers.

Mrs. Clara Peller was the "Where's the Beef?" lady. Her commercials, in which she asked a hamburger fast-food cook, "Where's the beef?" inspired Candidate Walter Mondale to ask the same question of his opponent, Gary Hart. (Wendy's Old Fashioned Hamburgers)

Mr. Mondale leaned over toward Mr. Hart once during a candidate debate and said, "Where's the beef? That's what I'm asking." Everyone understood immediately that Mondale was hinting that Hart had no "beef" in his ideas. And it hurt Hart's campaign a lot, too, since the idea of low content seemed to stick. Mondale won the nomination, although he lost the election to Ronald Reagan.

Once you put the "beef" together and have a good set of ideas to offer people, you have to make sure that they understand what you are talking about. In other words, you have to be able to *communicate*. President Ronald Reagan, elected in 1980 and 1984 by huge margins, is considered one of the best communicators in presidential history. In fact, reporters had a nickname for him: the Great Communicator. Even when he had ideas that people might have resisted under ordinary circumstances, he was so good at delivering those ideas to people that they accepted them.

Even congressmen and senators who disagreed with him often voted his way in the first years of his presidency, because they were afraid that if they didn't, they might make the voters mad and lose their own elections next time. That's the power that comes with good communication!

Another person who showed how much the communication of ideas influences politics was Franklin Delano Roosevelt, who was president during the Great Depression and World War II. He was elected four times, more than any other American president, because he could make people believe that he could lead the country forward during some of the roughest moments in its history.

Through radio addresses, especially when he gave *fire-side chats,* so named because he sat next to the White House fireplace as he spoke, he reassured the nation and helped people to believe that, despite the desperate problems of Depression and war, things would get better. His gift for encouraging people was admired by politicians in both parties, including Ronald Reagan, whose ideas on government were very different, but who quoted Roosevelt often.

President Franklin Delano Roosevelt, the only president ever to serve four terms in office, giving one of his fireside chats. Historians believe that these radio addresses helped to hold the country together during very tough times, as the Depression of the 1930s led into World War II. (Wide World Photos, Inc.)

Roosevelt spoke to people on the radio. There was no TV then. Reagan's speeches appeared on TV newscasts. These days, if a national candidate doesn't have the skills to speak on TV, he is going to have a tough time winning an election.

TV communication requires special talents. You have to speak calmly and with a warmth and intimacy that you never needed when campaigning consisted mostly of big public gatherings and rallies. In effect, you need not only ideas and the ability to communicate them, you also need to be able to do that communicating on television. As you'll see later, the need for TV skills has built an industry of its own.

A Real Race

Now you have your message, and ideas you believe in, and you have learned how to get those ideas across to the voters. But you have to *reach* those voters so they will pay attention to your message. How do you do that? You need three big sets of tools: a smart political staff, the money and equipment that staff needs in order to operate, and a strategy that makes the best use of both those people and that equipment.

Let's look at the problem by pretending that you are running for Congress from the suburb of a big city. How are you going to win? Let's pretend that there is no *incumbent*—that is, no one is in the job now because the person who held that seat, or position, is retiring. The reason you are seeking an *open seat,* one with no one holding office, is that it is so tough to beat an incumbent that you have to use special tactics.

Think about it this way: if someone suddenly offered your family the chance to move to a new house, and told you that your new home would be bigger and better, but that you weren't allowed to see it until after you had decided whether to move or not, you might decide to stay in your old neighborhood just to be on the safe side. That's the same problem a person challenging an incumbent has: unless there is something really wrong with the current office-holder, it is tough to beat him. People tend to stick with the person they know unless that guy is a real disaster.

So here you are with an opportunity to be elected to the House of Representatives. You know what you want to do and what you think is important. How do you get yourself elected so that you can do it?

First Things First

You had better organize a staff so that you can get everything else done. Of course you need a *campaign manager* who knows how to put the rest of the staff together. But just as early, you will need a *fund-raiser* who can go out into the community and make sure that you have enough money to pay the campaign manager, and the rest of the staff, to rent offices and pay the phone bills (campaigns really use a lot of telephones) and the electric bills, to pay the printer for the posters and the buttons, and to pay for all the other things we're going to talk about, too.

Fund-raising is a real skill. Sometimes a candidate can get attention for his campaign just by letting it be known that a certain professional fund-raiser has agreed to help. But fund-raising can also be done by ordinary people. You know that if you've ever had a bake sale or washed cars to raise money for a school trip.

Raising money for a campaign isn't all that different. People may give small parties where the candidate comes to speak. Guests pay for the tickets, or else get phone calls from volunteers who ask them for money after the party is over. Sometimes famous people will agree to come to a party for a candidate just so people will buy tickets to get to meet them. Movies stars do that a lot. Rock stars and country singers sometimes give concerts to help, too. And often there are other creative ways to raise money. Campaigns sell buttons, tote bags, banners, and posters. They send out mailings to interested people. Sometimes they have small gatherings for very influential people so they will go out and seek money from their influential friends.

But whatever way you use, if you are running for office, you have to have money. In 1984, in the five most expensive Senate races, for example, each vote cast cost the candidates seven dollars and fifty cents! Most of that was for statewide TV advertising, which you may not choose to spend in our imaginary congressional race, but it sure is a lot of money. There is an old saying: "Money is the mother's milk of politics." And you know how far a growing baby would get without milk!

You should know, though, that because there have been problems in the past, there are laws about how much money one person can give to a candidate. If you're lucky enough to be rich, you may spend as much of your own money as you want during your campaign, though you have to be careful you don't spend so much that you look like a spoiled brat trying to buy yourself a job.

But if you have a rich uncle, you can't just go to him and ask for enough money to pay for everything. That's not allowed in any federal race. He and every other "private citizen" has a limit on how much he can give you.

You also have to file a list of all your contributors with the *Federal Elections Commission,* and all the contributors' names are public information. That's to try to help keep elections fair and to let voters know just what sorts of people are helping to pay for a campaign. The lists are available in Washington and are often published in the newspaper.

Why would you want to know who has contributed to which campaign? Suppose you are against the dumping of certain waste in rivers. If your opponent got a contribution from the officer of a company that was doing the dumping, or from a waste disposal company that made money on river cleanups, it would help you to know that.

If you want to ban skateboards within the city limits— except in designated areas—and your opponent gets contributions from a skateboard manufacturer, you need to know that. It doesn't mean that your opponent is selling his support, or promising to allow skateboards in the city if he gets the contribution. But it does mean that the people who would like to sell more skateboards think that this candidate is more sympathetic to them.

Lawmakers hope that by making contributions limited and public, the "selling" of support for various issues will not be a part of our government. And campaign managers read the lists, too. If a candidate gets money from someone unsavory or unpopular, the opponent's campaign will use that information against him in speeches and advertising.

Actress Ally Sheedy helps raise presidential campaign money
for Governor Mike Dukakis of Massachusetts in 1987. By
appearing at a party with a candidate, actors and other stars
get fans to buy tickets to the party too. That's one way candidates can raise money to run their campaigns. Most candidates
have *some* stars who are willing to show up at parties like this
one. (© 1987 Richard Sobel)

Not all the problems are solved, though. Since limits
have been put on how much one person, or one corporation
or union for that matter, can give to a single candidate,
people have found ways to give more money anyway. One

way is by forming a *political action committee* or *PAC*. These are groups of people or companies or organizations who join together to contribute to a campaign that affects their particular interests. Each person or company contributes money to the PAC and the committee then decides where to spend it. The members of a Senate Committee on Agriculture might get support from a PAC made up of various fertilizer industry people. Someone on the Labor Committee might get large contributions from a labor union PAC.

In your suburb, for example, suppose there is a big fight about where to allow new gas stations. Some people may be worried that those big underground gas tanks will leak into the water supply. They will want to keep the gas stations out of town. Others may feel that they have to drive too far to get gas, so they will want gas stations to be closer to their neighborhoods. It would be possible for an oil company political action committee to give a lot of money to the candidate who wants to allow gas stations into the neighborhood and for the political action committee for clean water to give a lot of money to the opponent of those gas stations.

PACs are limited in how much they can give to a candidate too, but both PACs and individuals may also make less restricted donations to state, local, and national parties, which may then spend that money to help candidates of their choice. Even with these loopholes, it is still tougher than it used to be to "buy" an election—just because you know more rich people than the other guy.

Presidential campaigns have gotten another boost from Congress. Federal law now allows every taxpayer to *check off* a little box on his Federal Income Tax return. If you

Form 1040
Department of the Treasury—Internal Revenue Service
U.S. Individual Income Tax Return 1986 (O)

For the year January 1-December 31, 1986, or other tax year beginning	, 1986, ending	, 19	OMB No. 1545-0074

Use IRS label. Other- wise, please print or type.	Your first name and initial (if joint return, also give spouse's name and initial)	Last name	Your social security number
	Present home address (number and street or rural route). (If you have a P.O. Box, see page 4 of Instructions.)		Spouse's social security number
	City, town or post office, state, and ZIP code	If this address is different from the one shown on your 1985 return, check here ▶	

| Presidential Election Campaign ▶ | Do you want $1 to go to this fund? | Yes | No | **Note:** *Checking "Yes" will not change your tax or reduce your refund.* |
| | If joint return, does your spouse want $1 to go to this fund? | Yes | No | |

As you can see, the Internal Revenue Service makes it easy for taxpayers to help finance presidential campaigns.

check off the box, one dollar of your taxes will go into a fund to "match" all money raised by presidential candidates up to a certain limit. For every dollar the candidates raise, the government will kick in a dollar too.

In exchange, the candidates must agree to a spending limit for their campaigns. Lawmakers hope that this method will help to keep things honest and to keep costs down.

Looking Good on the Campaign Trail

All the money in the world won't help your campaign if it doesn't run well, though, so you'd better find experts in another important area—the *advance staff*. Those are the people who show up at a campaign stop or speaking engagement "in advance"—hours or maybe even days before you, the candidate, get there.

The advance person will check out the size of the room, make sure the microphone is working and that there are no embarrassing signs around, see if there might be another group meeting nearby that day that could provide an easy extra appearance, and generally make sure that everything will work out when you arrive.

A good advance person will also get the names of everyone sitting up on the stage of the luncheon or rally you are addressing, so that you can mention each of them. She will give you a notecard with each person's name and role. Then you can thank them and make some complimentary comment about each of them. She'll also make sure that if there is some sticky issue you ought to know about, you don't get surprised. In politics, you never want to be surprised.

Why? Suppose you are going to a Lion's Club lunch to speak and to ask for support. Just suppose that two of the members are in a race for president of that chapter of the Lions and that the issue is whether to admit women to the club. You had better know in advance that you will be asked about women being allowed to join private clubs, and you had better be prepared with a good answer, or you are going to lose more votes than you gain.

In presidential and state-wide campaigns, advance people have even more responsibility. TV and newspaper reporters are going to be following the candidates around. That means everything has to go smoothly and look good or it is going to seem as though the candidate can't even manage his campaign, much less the job he's running for. If the advance man doesn't round up a big crowd, it will look as though no one is interested in the person who is running. If the advance man doesn't have some neat music or a few famous people to speak at the rally, it might be boring and not get on the news that night.

Even in your congressional race your advance person has to be sure that you are in the right places at the right times and that the people most important in that community are persuaded to show up and welcome you, so that others in the community think you are worth voting for. Then when you communicate your message effectively, as you have learned to do, people will be ready, even excited, to hear it.

Is Anybody Listening?

While you are deciding how to communicate that message, you also need to know which part of your message to stress. And you need to know if you are getting across to the voters. So another sort of person you want to hire is a *pollster*. A pollster is a person, or group of people, who do telephone or face-to-face opinion surveys during the election season. They will ask questions like, "If the election were held today, would you be most likely to vote for candidate ———— or ———— or ————?"

They ask a lot of issues-related questions too, so they can see if the candidate or the issues is more important to the voters. They keep track by age and sex, so they see if the candidate does better with older voters or younger ones, with men or with women, etc. All of this information helps a campaign to adjust to the wishes of the voters, if the polling is done accurately by competent people. Polls give the voters a chance to let their candidates know what they want, too, and that is also valuable.

It is never perfect, of course. Sometimes people get embarrassed to tell what they really think, and, instead, tell a pollster what they think they ought to think. Sometimes

Student volunteers in a boiler room in New Hampshire.
(Cynthia K. Samuels)

people just plain change their minds. But polls really do help a campaign to keep up with the voters.

You as the candidate have to be strong, though. You may want to adjust your message to reach more people, or make commercials to work on your image if you learn from the polls that people have some doubts about your abilities.

The problem arises when you find out that the voters in your district are against gun registration, and you really feel that it is important. Or they oppose a Supreme Court nomination whom you know you would support. In other words, you learn that voters feel differently from you on a big issue.

At times like those, you have a hard choice. You can change your position to suit the voters, of course. But if the issue is a big one with a base in moral or ethical philosophy, like gun control, voters might just end up not trusting you at all, instead of liking you better for going their way.

So you have to decide whether to say to the voters, "I know how you feel but I couldn't be honorable if I voted the way you want. So let me explain why I believe as I do, and you can elect me or not." Or you can risk changing to please the voters. But would you respect someone who did that?

In New York State, two governors in a row were opposed to the death penalty. Both Governor Hugh Carey and Governor Mario Cuomo believed it was wrong for the state to take a life, even from a killer. Cuomo even had public arguments with his mother when he was running because she supported capital punishment.

In each governor's term the state legislature passed a popular death penalty bill. Each governor vetoed the bill and kept it from becoming law in New York. Both were popular and respected leaders, so people accepted their unpopular position and reelected them anyway.

Turning to the Experts

Sometimes when you run into a problem on a "pesky" issue like the death penalty or gun control, you can solve it by being very creative or different in your approach. And these days there is another whole category of people you need to consider if you are running for office—professionals who can help you deal with such problems. They are called *campaign consultants,* and there are many of them around to chose from. Their inclusion in your campaign will mean, of course, that you need to raise enough money to pay them.

What do they do? Well, they take all the information about your election district and the polls that your polling office has done, and they use that information to help you plan your campaign. Just how should you handle that toughest of all issues in your district? How hard should you be on your opponent? Which of the issues you care the most about should you stress? If your opponent is getting too old to be in office, should you say so, or is he so popular you will only hurt your campaign if you do? Should you use TV advertising, or in your area is radio and direct mail better?

If you are a man and your wife uses her own last name, should she change it to yours to please voters who don't like to see women being that independent? (One governor really *did* ask his wife to take his name after many years of using her own. He had been elected once and then lost reelection because people thought he was too ambitious. They thought he only wanted to be governor so he could move on to another job like senator or president. In a way, her use of his name was symbolic. It meant that the two of them were listening to the state's more conservative voters, and the change helped him to be elected again!)

Often the most important thing consultants do is to make TV commercials. If they are good ones, they help to make the candidate's positions on issues clearer and more appealing to the voter. If they are less scrupulous or honorable, the commercials may be only attacks on or mockeries of an opponent, or simple little complimentary profiles of the candidate that tell the voters nothing.

Some campaign consultants come complete with TV

commercials staff, polling staff, and advance advisors. They also provide people who can plan your campaign strategy. Though many are highly regarded, some candidates prefer to keep more control over their campaigns by hiring different groups to do different jobs.

Of course, when you are facing a tough issue, or a problem in your campaign that is likely to get a lot of news coverage, you have yet another important staff member to consider: your *press secretary*. In fact, the press secretary is important both to interpret your position on tough issues to the press and to make sure that you get as much coverage as your opponent—or better yet, even more. He is also the person who takes interview requests, who calls local reporters to tell them you will be having a news conference, who writes press releases and generally sees to your public image.

Sometimes it can be a very complicated job. Suppose you have taken a position that is very controversial, and reporters are trying to find out if you will stick to it. It is the press secretary who is your ambassador to the reporters and makes sure that they write and broadcast the most important things about your reasoning and position.

Get the Idea?

In addition to those who run your campaign, you need some people to help organize your ideas correctly. In the "message" department, there are two important groups. One is your *speech writers*. The other is your *issues staff*. Depending on the size of the campaign budget, you may be able to afford to hire people just to do research on issues for you. You may divide them into *domestic* and *foreign,* or, in a House race like yours, you may decide you can't afford foreign issues people.

At any rate, the domestic people will study issues like hunger, homelessness, environmental problems, school funding, and other problems in the United States. The foreign staff, if you hire one, will be more concerned with our country's role abroad. Where should we send troops? How should we decide which governments to be friends with? How should we deal with the Russians?

In presidential campaigns, there are huge staffs to deal with each of these issues, but in your congressional campaigns you'll probably have one or two people. And if you are lucky, maybe some local experts who like your ideas will volunteer to do some of the issues work for you because they want you to win.

People who care about the issues that a particular candidate is stressing often volunteer to work in his campaign. A good way to practice before running for office is to volunteer in somebody else's campaign first.

Once your issues workers have begun putting together information, you can set your positions. But then you may want your speech writers to help you figure out the best way to tell people what you think. Speech writers are very good at finding phrases that make your case in the best possible way. Of course, you can change what they give you, but they can save a lot of time, writing one speech for a women's rights group, one for an environmental group, one for a judges' and lawyers' association, and another for bankers. Even so, many candidates would rather write their own speeches. Others prefer to speak from notes and never write the whole speech down at all, even when there are many different groups to consider.

Each of these groups, and all the others you will speak to, will expect you to speak about issues that interest them, and what you would do about them. Teachers worry about school funding and teachers' rights; environmental groups worry about pollution, bankers worry about interest rates and inflation, and lawyers and judges worry about law enforcement. You have to worry about all of those things, since as a congressperson you will have to cast informed votes in every area.

One Person Who Did It

Lynn Martin,

Republican of Illinois,
who started as a teacher and a mom, and became
a congresswoman and a leader in her party

Representative Lynn Martin is a mother of two who began her working life as a high school teacher. When she decided that the local politicians in her hometown of Rockford were not in touch with the needs of the community, she ran for the county board herself, and she won.

Four years later, she ran for a seat in the Illinois State House, and won again. Many of her supporters were the junior high school friends of one of her daughters. The kids went door to door to help gain support for Mrs. Martin and they did a good job.

In 1980, Congressman John Anderson decided to run a third party presidential campaign (remember page 34?). Martin decided to seek his House seat, which would be open since he wasn't allowed to run for president and run for the House at the same time. She won the nomination for Congress and was elected.

As a respected member of the House and of her party, Martin serves as vice chairman of the House Republican Conference. That's a leadership post where decisions about day-to-day operations in Congress are made. She is the first woman to hold that post, and her supporters believe she will continue to move up.

Observers note that she takes on real challenges, including service on such difficult committees in the House as

Representative Lynn Martin and her daughters, Julia [center]
and Caroline [right], outside the Capitol in Washington.
(Office of Rep. Lynn Martin)

the Armed Services and Budget committees. Both of them
take a lot of homework. Her hard work has been rewarded.
She was asked to second the nomination of George Bush
as vice president at the 1984 Republican convention. That
speech put her on television at a time when lots of people
were watching. News magazines have recognized her as
one of the top ten rising stars in American politics.

Chapter 8
Tools of the Trade

Now you have this wonderful staff to run and organize your campaign. And because your fund-raiser was good, and we know you are a good candidate, you have money. But you are nowhere near having a real campaign yet! You need some tools for this talented professional staff to use.

The first tool that you need is an *organization*. Take a look at a county map if you can find one. Maybe there are some in your school library. You will see that your area is divided into streets and neighborhoods. Each of those neighborhoods is built around a couple of institutions. In some, it may be a church or a school. In some, it may be a park or playground that everyone helped to build; or a swimming pool, or a factory where everyone works.

You want your staff to be able to reach potential voters efficiently. By figuring out which are the primary institutions in your community, and using them, you can build an organization. Maybe you will go speak or pass out leaflets at church or town meetings. Maybe you will go to the factory when the shifts change to shake hands and to invite people to work in your campaign and to vote for you. If your advance people do a good job, and the workers know you are coming, you can get to a lot of people that way.

Does That Compute?

The most efficient way to build an organization today is with the help of a *computer*. Neither advance people nor telephones nor lists made at town meetings or church groups will be as effective as they might be unless you have a computer. There are so many ways to use computers in a campaign that they could make a book by themselves. Some of the most obvious are: to keep track of issues raised by voters at town meetings and factory gates, to computerize the list of registered voters that is always available at the board of elections, to generate a list of phone numbers for likely voters; to organize information from the polls your pollster took; to figure out if the people you need to reach are TV watchers or whether TV ads would be a waste of time and money, and to analyze by the direct mail lists from your district what issues interest voters the most.

For example, suppose you program into the computer the number of National Rifle Association members, the number of teachers, the number of people with kids under six, and the number of old people. Then you could figure out whether you need to pay more attention to gun control (National Rifle people), daycare (parents of small kids), education funding (teachers), or social security (old folks).

You can also put church or school or garden club lists into the computer to add to your base. Suppose you want to run on environmental issues. Before you announce that you are running you will want to go speak to the garden clubs and nature societies near you to get supporters and volunteers. Dump their names and addresses into your computer and you have the beginnings of a corps of really supportive workers and fund-raisers.

If you are a veteran of the military, you want to try and build a similar base by using lists of other veterans. If people at the neighborhood factory are worried that it might close, or that foreign competition may hurt their product, that plant and its union membership roster is especially good as a tool to recruit supporters. All of these groups are easier to reach, no matter what the issue, if they are computerized *by issue* as well as by neighborhood.

If it's the sort of neighborhood with church or union picnics, even better. Show up and shake hands and get names and addresses to build that neighborhood organization we've been talking about—and put those names into the computer.

Why? Because on election day one of the most important things you will have to do is to *get out the vote*. If your organization is built around neighborhoods, volunteers can offer rides to the polls to those who might not have a way to get there, or child care while they go vote. They may be able to find out who in the neighborhood will be away during the elections, and to make sure those people get *absentee ballots*. (These are ballots you mail in in advance if you won't be in town on election day. By making sure your candidate's supporters vote absentee, you get some extra votes.)

If you are going to have volunteers knock on doors to see how your campaign is coming and to pass out literature, or if you plan to do that yourself, you need to have everything broken down by street and neighborhood so you don't miss any big areas, or, just as bad, go to the same house too many times and annoy the people you are trying to win over. Computers can help you plan that, too.

Phone Power

You can add a lot to your organization with another tool treasured by political operators. It's one you know very well: the telephone. Any campaign that can afford it will set up a *phone bank,* what's called a *boiler room.* That's a room with a lot of telephones so that staffers or volunteers can work the phones to get support. They may call registered voters to be sure that people plan to get out and vote, or to raise money if you start to run short, or to recruit volunteers.

The best way for you to use the phone bank in a race for Congress is to figure out all the telephone prefixes in the congressional district where you are running. Put them into the computer and generate phone lists for your volunteers. That way you are only calling people in your district.

The callers in turn will rate each person they speak to and enter into the computer just how responsive those people are. Probably they would do this by using a little script. They might say "Hello. My name is ——— and I am working for the congressional campaign of John Doe. Could I take a minute of your time?" The script would go on to give the best possible way of asking for volunteers or of asking people if they need a ride to the polls or if there is an issue they feel particularly strongly about. As the elections draw closer the phone banks become more and more valuable to keep people aware of the campaign and to make them feel that the candidate cares about them.

If you have enough volunteers and can afford enough phones, you can contact every voter in your district and rate them, then program the computer to list them five through one in each neighborhood. The ones who hate your candidate would get a one, those who love the candidate would get a five. In-betweens would get a two, three, or four.

Think what you could do with those lists! Before election day you could send supporters to work on the threes and try to turn them into stronger supporters, and to encourage the fours. You could recruit the fives to be volunteers. On election day you would know which ones to seek out to vote, and which ones to leave alone.

Postal Politics

Besides the telephone, there is another tool to make voters feel that the candidate is interested in them. It's called *direct mail*. You've probably gotten plenty of that in your house. If you get *Baseball Digest* and discover that *Sporting News* has written to you to see if you want a subscription, or if you order a cassette or record in the mail and suddenly receive offers from all sorts of record clubs, you are getting direct, or *targeted mail*.

The people who want to sell something to you have bought the mailing list of a company that already knows you are interested in their product. If you get *Baseball Digest*, you probably like sports, right? If you order records in the mail, you like music. So it is worth it to a company to buy the list of subscribers to the magazine or record clubs and *target* them for future purchases.

Same with politics. Certain magazines, for example, have a political point of view. The *National Review* is conservative; the *Nation* is very liberal. Which mailing list would help a conservative candidate find supporters? The *National Review,* right?

These mailing lists can also come from contributions to charities. If you contribute to the National Wildlife Federation, you probably are interested in the environment. If you donate to the American Cancer Society, you are likely interested in health issues. As you can imagine, even local races can use these lists, if they can afford them. Since computers can break the lists down by zip codes, it's pretty easy to buy only those that apply to your area. Charities and organizations, even magazine publishers, often make extra money by selling their mailing lists.

Of similar value when organizing support are organizations to whom one issue is most important. Maybe they are *labor unions* who want to be sure that their right to organize is protected. Maybe they are movie companies who are concerned about video rental regulations, or real estate dealers worried about property taxes. Sometimes professional groups, like the *American Medical Association,* the *National Education Association,* or the *National Farm Board,* may form interest groups to support candidates who will look after their interests and ideas.

One name for these groups, who might vote for someone they dislike on other matters if they can get them to agree on their special issue, is *single-issue groups.* They have a great influence in American politics because they can get all the people who feel as they do to vote along with them.

They have their membership *mailing lists,* too, and can reach interested people quickly that way.

Of course, a candidate must have the money to buy a list in the first place, but once he can afford the list, he is able to reach people who feel strongly about the things he cares about. It's an efficient way to reach the voters most likely to like you, so these lists have become very valuable and direct mail is now a political profession of its own, just as it is in the sale of magazine subscriptions or record clubs.

TV Talents

At least as important as the other tools we've been discussing is one hard to define: your television image. You already know that you need to be a good television speaker to look good; you have to answer questions briefly and clearly so your answers can be used on the news, and you need to be calm and reasonable in TV appearances. You also need to understand how TV works.

First of all, television is obviously a visual medium. You look at it. So even if you have wonderful things to say, you have to say them in a way that uses the "looking." And to be a responsible candidate you also have to try to make sure that your television appearances and commercials are more than just "pretty pictures." It is certainly tempting to have a commercial show a candidate walking along the beach with a dog, the wind blowing gently behind them. Candidates look nice that way. But voters don't learn very much from this kind of commercial about what the candidates will do or help to do if he or she is elected.

Here is a commercial that showed nice pictures but

MISSING CHILDREN: A campaign commercial from 1986
(The Communications Company, Washington, D.C.)

1. EVERYTIME WE KISS THEM
   GOOD-BYE,

2. A SMALL PART OF US FEARS
   IT COULD BE FOR THE
   LAST TIME.

5. PAUL SIMON CARES DEEPLY
   ABOUT OUR FAMILIES,

6. SO HE WROTE AND PASSED
   A LAW MAKING IT

3. EACH DAY IN AMERICA, MORE THAN

4. 3,000 CHILDREN DISAPPEAR. SOME NEVER COME HOME.

PAUL SIMON
A Senator We Can Count On

7. EASIER TO FIND MISSING CHILDREN AND RETURN THEM HOME.

8. PAUL SIMON. A SENATOR WE CAN COUNT ON.

also told voters something good. (Commercials always tell you something good about the guy paying for the commercial, right?)

Senator Paul Simon really did help to write the missing kids legislation, and that commercial evoked deep feelings about the issue of missing children, but it also gave you some information. Good commercials do that. Learn to be a critical voter by noticing just what sorts of commercials candidates choose to make.

Watch some election commercials and learn to decide for yourself whether you are watching something that helps you make a decision or something that plays on your emotions and tries to manipulate you. If there is a real heavy-duty issue in your state or town, watch how it is handled in the commercials and see if you think the candidate was well advised by his consultants and pollsters.

Big News

TV isn't just commercials, though. In the city near the suburb where you are running, there are radio and TV stations. If you get on the news, like Governor Graham did with his work days, you get free publicity even if you can't afford many television commercials. So when you are organizing your campaign schedule, plan some visual events (often called "photo opportunities") that will be sure to get you on TV.

If you support daycare, go visit some daycare centers and make sure the TV stations know you are going. If you think drugs are a big danger, go to some drug rehab places, or go talk to a group of Scouts about drugs, and see if you can get the stations to cover you there. Again, the free media coverage you will get will make you more familiar to the voters and get your points across.

But if the reporters on the scene ask you questions, there is another very important skill that you need. If you want to be on the television news, you have to talk in short sentences called "soundbites." Most news shows use short clips of people talking. No news show is very long, so it can't spend too much time on one thing. TV news producers love politicians who talk in twenty-second "bites." Today, the candidate who can offer clever, short bites is the candidate who will most likely get on television.

People Power

As valuable as television and radio are, though, nothing replaces people. A human tool in your campaign is the *volunteer*. People often volunteer to work for free in political campaigns if the candidate is someone they believe in. You may think that with computers and television you don't need people anymore. But you're wrong. Since people do the voting, they need to be a part of the process. And in a congressional race like yours, where you can't spend money the way a presidential candidate would, people can do what the money would have done.

Need to get the voters organized by issue and can't afford a computer to go through your lists? Volunteers can do it. They can drive people to the polls, make sure that those rallies that will be covered for TV are well attended, and, before voters know who you are, volunteers can pass out leaflets and buttons to make sure your name becomes a part of things.

Volunteers are also voters. So when you build a huge group of volunteers, you are guaranteeing yourself some highly committed voters, all of whom have spouses and neighbors and work colleagues and friends. If they are working in your campaign they will try even harder to make sure their friends vote for you too, because it will make them successful in their efforts. If you succeed, so do they.

Young people are very valuable volunteers even before they are old enough to vote. It's not just that voters are impressed with a candidate who will make room for young people in his campaign. Young volunteers also learn the system and become more informed voters and better citizens later; they are the next generation of voters. By the time you get tired of your House seat and decide to run for the Senate, they'll be ready to vote for you!

There's something to remember, though, as you read this inventory of important tools to campaign with: there's really only one thing you need to win an election: *votes!* Sometimes candidates get so carried away with technique that they forget that. Allard Lowenstein, Eugene McCarthy, and the others who worked in 1968 stopped Lyndon Johnson with primitive efforts, but with total devotion to an idea. Any person who cares enough about an issue to work to gather those votes may find new ways to reach voters. Maybe your race will be the one to create a whole new campaign style.

One Person Who Did It

John Lewis,

Democrat of Georgia,
who faced angry mobs, police chiefs, and fear as he led
civil rights demonstrations in the South

John Lewis has probably been in jail more than any other member of Congress. He's been beaten up more times, too.

When he was twenty-three years old, Lewis was the youngest of the six leaders of the great 1963 civil rights march on Washington. As coordinator of the Student Nonviolent Coordinating Committee, he risked his life, his health, and his future in the bloodiest years of the American civil rights movement in the South.

In those days, it was pretty tough to be a civil rights leader and not face arrest and beatings and abuse. But Lewis had been inspired by Dr. Martin Luther King when he was young. One of ten children of a sharecropper, he had wanted to be a minister, but became involved in the civil rights movement instead. He was determined to end southern laws that kept blacks and whites separate and denied equal rights to black Americans.

His determination led him to dozens of marches and sit-ins. As he faced down angry southern whites and policemen, he was beaten unconscious four times and arrested more than forty. But he kept on in his quest for justice for all Americans.

For several years he supervised the Voter Education Project in Atlanta, and then in 1977 he ran for Congress and lost. President Carter appointed him head of ACTION, a federal department that helped the poor here in the United States.

In 1981 he was elected to the Atlanta City Council, where he served until he was elected to the House of Representatives in 1986.

Civil rights activist John Lewis is arrested during a demonstration in Nashville, Tennessee, in 1964. Lewis was arrested more than forty times but never gave up. (Wide World Photos, Inc.)

Congressman John Lewis, 1987. Many of the people who got the right to vote through the civil rights activism of men like Lewis later helped to elect him Congressman from Atlanta. (Office of Rep. John Lewis)

Chapter 9

Why Should I Care and What Can I Do?

By now you must have realized that elections are not only about things like unemployment and nuclear arms: things that may seem very far away or too big for you to deal with. Political issues determine what happens in your life almost every day. And the issues are decided by the people who get elected.

The people who decide which textbooks you get in school are either elected officials or are hired by an elected official. And who do you think decides if your town or city will have curfews for kids under sixteen? People who run for office and get elected. They may even have gotten elected by promising to impose curfews on kids.

Most of the things in your life that your parents don't decide are decided by lawmakers or school officials. School boards are elected, and hire principals, who hire teachers. City councils are elected and decide the rules for your town. State legislatures are elected and set the rules for drinking age, drivers' licenses, and work permits.

The Supreme Court says that the Constitution gives adults the right to protect kids—even though kids *do* have some rights, too. But these two kinds of rights are always bumping into each other, so if you want a say in just *how* adults decide to protect you, you might want to pay attention to who gets elected to make the laws.

What You Can Do If You Want to Help

No election is too small to need help, and you don't have to be old enough to vote to be old enough to work in a campaign. If there is something you care a lot about, whether it is money for the marching band or neighborhood safety, there are sure to be people running for office who care, or can be made to care, about the same things.

Young people work to sign up volunteers for a Long Island, New York, congressional campaign. (Southern Historical Collection, University of North Carolina at Chapel Hill)

Candidates want us to support them because we agree with the things they believe, with their positions on the issues. As we watch them try to win our support, we should remember that once the fun is over and they've won the job, our lives will be affected by what those winners do.

Find out what part of the government is in charge of the things you care most about. Figure out who is running for those jobs. Then find out what their position is on your issue. You can always call a campaign office and ask. You can also read the papers and watch news on TV to figure it out.

After you decide whom to support, there is plenty for you to do. You can answer phones at headquarters and take messages. You can sell buttons and campaign stuff to raise money. You can go door to door with leaflets and information to save postage, so the campaign can spend the money somewhere else. You can work on phone banks.

On election day you can baby-sit for people so they can go vote, or you can help hand out pamphlets at the polling place. Many candidates have youth committees, too.

It's been said that people who don't vote get what they deserve. The same thing is true of people who don't pay attention to the election issues or to who is on the ticket. If you think that those old enough to be drafted or to vote should be allowed to drink legally; if you believe that student loans for colleges are important or that the United States should send more money to the homeless or spend more on defense, then you have to know which elected officials think the same way you do. And if they don't, you have to know how to get them out of office.

But in most elections, fewer than forty percent of eligi-

John F. Kennedy in a 1960 motorcade. (Burton Berinsky)

ble voters even bother to vote. Around fifteen percent more vote in presidential elections. Among eighteen-to-twenty-one-year-old voters, who only got the right to vote in 1971, the numbers are even lower than that!

Lots of people think that the world is so big, and the American system is so complicated, that they can't do anything to change it. But there is a secret about the huge system that we live under. It is made up of people, one after the other. Whether they are town clerks or high school principals, voters or police chiefs, student volunteers or highly paid political coordinators, the American system works the same way for all of them. Or at least it should.

All it takes is for all of us to remember that politics is the way people get into and keep the jobs that affect our lives. If we don't keep an eye on things and help to elect the people who will do things the way we want them done, then we deserve to be disappointed.

It's a lot more work to live in a country where the people are in charge. This book is called *It's a Free Country* because the only way we can keep it that way is to pay better attention to the decisions that get made here and to how they get made. We already have the rights. Now we just have to get our act together and use them.

Glossary

Absentee ballots: Ballots distributed in advance to voters who know that they will be away on election day. They are allowed to fill in these ballots and mail them in even though they are absent on the day of the election.

Acclamation: With everyone agreeing. To be nominated by acclamation is to have everyone who is voting agree that you should be nominated.

Accountable: Required to answer for actions and decisions. Politicians are accountable to the voters and can be defeated for reelection if they can't explain to voters exactly why they voted as they did.

Advance staff: Campaign staff members who set up candidate appearances in advance so that everything goes smoothly when the candidate arrives.

American Medical Association: A professional organization of doctors that represents their interests to the public.

Balance the ticket: To find a way to combine candidates so that different interests are all represented. For example, a liberal candidate might balance the ticket with a more conservative running mate; a northerner with a southern resident.

Boiler room: A nickname for the room where telephone operations like polling or fund-raising phone calls are carried out.

Bosses: Political party leaders with power over the political, and sometimes personal, lives of people in their neighborhoods.

Campaign consultant: A professional campaign organizer who helps to decide campaign strategy and tactics and knows how to use polling and commercials most effectively.

Campaign manager: Overall supervisor of a campaign.

Candidate: A person running for office.

Caucuses: Meetings of party members held so that they can make decisions of joint interest.

C.D.: The nickname for congressional district.

Check-off: A blank on an income-tax return that permits a tax payer to designate one dollar of his taxes to help finance the presidential elections.

Communicate: To make sure one's ideas are understood and accepted.

Computer: A machine used to efficiently organize and use information. Usually computers can perform routine sorting and ordering much more quickly than the human mind.

Congressional district: A legally set area represented by a congressman.

Conservative: A political point of view. Often, conservatives believe that local governments are most effective and that too much "big government" hurts democracy. Conservatives are often extra suspicious of the Soviet Union and of high taxes or big spending programs.

Convention: A party gathering, often to nominate candidates from that party to run in various elections.

Convention delegates: Representatives to a convention. The number of delegates per state is determined by the state's population.

Deadlock: A tie vote that does not appear to be breakable. The vote is deadlocked if no voter in a tie will change his vote.

Declare: To announce that one is a candidate for office.

Delegate: Representative to a convention.

Delegation: A group of representatives from one state or district.

Democrats: One of two major political parties in the United States.

Direct election: An election in which the votes cast elect the winner directly.

Direct mail: Mail sent to people who are on targeted lists made up of people with particular interests or ideas in common, like labor or environmental issues.

District: The geographic area a representative is responsible for and elected by.

Dixiecrats: Southern politicians who pulled out of the Democratic party in 1948 and started their own Dixiecrat party so they could protest the sympathy that they believed Democrats were showing to blacks.

Domestic: At home. In government that means issues that have to do with things inside the United States.

Domino theory: The theory that an area or set of nations that border on one another can become Communist in the same way that one domino knocks down the one next to it, and that one knocks down the one after that. During the 1960s, it was this domino theory that drove Lyndon Johnson to continue the war in Vietnam for so long.

Electoral college: This group of people, whose numbers are determined by the results of a presidential election, meets after election day to formally cast the votes that elect the president. The winner of the presidential election in each state gets all of that state's votes when the electoral college meets.

Electors: The people who go to vote at the electoral college.

Factions: Conflicting interest groups within one organization. Often factions work against each other and cause problems.

Favorite son: A politician who runs for president from his home state even though he probably can't win. By holding his state's delegates' votes, he gains influence for both his state and himself.

Federal Elections Commission: A government commission that watches over elections to see that they are fair and enforces all the rules that Congress sets about how elections should work. The FEC also keeps all records on contributions to campaigns and investigates complaints when candidates feel they have been dealt with unfairly by their opponents.

Federal government: The government that presides over all the states, and whose laws and regulations apply to all states. Also called the national government.

Federal offices: Elected or appointed positions that are part of the federal government. Senators and congressmen hold federal offices.

Fireside chats: Radio broadcasts made by President Franklin Delano Roosevelt during the hard periods of the Depression and World War II. They were called fireside chats because he usually broadcast from beside a fireplace, either at the White House or at his home in Hyde Park, New York.

First ballot: The first vote for a nominee at a convention; the first time the delegates cast their votes for one nominee or another.

Floor fights: Battles on the floor of a convention hall or legislative chamber, in which two or more positions are disputed in public. Pressure is placed on delegates on the convention or congressional floor to vote one way or another.

Foreign: Having to do with matters outside a country's borders.

Fund-raiser: A person or event used to raise money for an election campaign.

General election: The election whose winners will serve in the offices for which they are running.

Gerrymandering: Manipulating the borders of congressional or other electoral districts so that the district is made up primarily of one party's voters.

Get out the vote: A term used to name the process of making sure that your supporters leave home and go vote on election day, instead of staying home because they're not interested or because they think you can win without them.

Governing: Presiding over a nation or other area of authority, enforcing the laws and tending to the operations and the services of that area.

Heading the ticket: Running for the highest office in a particular election. The candidate for president heads his party's ticket, for example.

Hearings: Meetings by a committee with authority to make decisions, such as a platform committee, so that committee members can hear various views before determining a policy.

Held the White House: Was president, or was the party to which the president belonged.

Horse trading: Making deals to get things done. Trading a "little this" for a "little that."

Incumbent: The person who is currently in office is the incumbent in that office.

Independent: A person who chooses not to belong to a political party is an independent.

Issues: Specific subjects or problems that voters care about.

Issues staff: Campaign staff people who help a candidate decide the best position to take on various issues.

Labor unions: Organizations of working people whose jobs are similar. Labor unions try to make working conditions and wages better for their members.

Landslide: A gigantic electoral victory very much like a huge slide of land, down a hill. When a candidate gets a huge majority of votes in an election, he has won by a landslide.

Liberals: Generally regarded as people whose political philosophy expects the federal government to be active in solving problems. Often, liberals are also seen as those who believe that spending more government money to help the poor is a good idea. Liberals often favor more individual decision making on private issues like sex, religion, or abortion.

Lieutenant governor: A deputy governor.

Local elections: Elections held to decide who will hold neighborhood or city or county offices.

Mailing lists: Lists of people who ought to get campaign mail asking for support. These lists are made up by finding areas that a candidate supports and then looking for other institu-

120 *It's a Free Country*

tions that might have lists of people who support the same things.

Major parties: The Democratic and Republican parties.

Markets: Areas that are reached by one city's TV or radio stations.

Message: A set of ideas that a candidate wants to communicate.

Movement: A group of people moving together to advance an idea or to change the way things happen.

National convention: Presidential nominating conventions held by each party to name their nominees for the national posts of president and vice president.

National Education Association: An organization of teachers that represents them in public and looks after their interests.

National Farm Board: A farm organization that represents the interests of some farmers.

Off-year elections: Federal elections held in nonpresidential years.

Old pols: Long-time professionals in politics.

Open seat: A congressional or senate seat for which there is no incumbent.

Organization: The party machinery and local staff, which make a campaign or political party function well.

PAC: A political action committee (see below)

Paid their dues: Spent time helping out in campaigns or political operations in order to gain the respect of political professionals.

Petition: A list of signatures of registered voters. The proper petitions will gain a candidate or party or issue a place on the ballot.

Phone bank: A set of telephones set up so a campaign worker can make organized phone calls to help elect a candidate.

Planks: Individual issue positions. All planks combine to form the platform.

Platform: A set of issue positions upon which a candidate or party will run.

Platform committee: A committee of party members that meets to hold hearings, hear positions, and determine the party platform.

Political action committee: An organization formed to raise money and to donate it to candidates with which the political action committee agrees. Also known as a *PAC.*

Politics: The art and tactics of getting elected to office and the skills and knowledge needed to be successful once elected.

Pollster: A person who takes opinion surveys to find out what people want, what they believe, and which candidates they like best.

Pols: Professional politicians, usually ones with a lot of power.

Press secretary: The person who represents the candidate or elected official in dealings with reporters and publicity.

Primaries or Primary elections: Elections in which candidates run for the right to run for office. Voters in the candidates' party vote among possible contenders.

Primary season: The months during which primary elections are held. Usually the primary season runs from February till early summer.

Private sector: Nongovernment work.

Proportion: Percentage.

Realignment: The transfer of majority status from one party to another.

Regional issues: Issues of concern to one geographic area that may look very different to another part of the country.

Register to vote: Sign up to be an eligible voter.

Registered voters: People who have signed up and are eligible to vote in elections.

Release: To allow convention delegates pledged to one candidate to vote for someone else instead. A candidate will release his delegates when he thinks he cannot win.

Republican party: One of the two major American political parties.

Roll call: The calling of the roll of delegations or representatives so that they may vote and have their votes registered.

Signatures: The names of registered voters, signed by those voters on nominating petitions. No candidate or party may appear on the ballot without a certain number of signatures.

Single-issue groups: Groups concerned with only one issue or area of interest.

Speech writers: People who write speeches for candidates.

State delegation: Group of delegates or representatives from one state.

State governments: The government of a state. Each of the fifty has a constitutionally guaranteed right to make laws and levy taxes on its own. State governments control many parts of our lives, like drinking age, working age, and driving regulations.

State legislature: The "congress" or set of representatives from one state.

State-wide races: Elections in which candidates must run in the whole state.

Straight party ticket: A list of candidates from the same party who are all running for different offices.

Superdelegate: A set of delegates to the Democratic convention who are not elected by any process but appointed by the party. They get to be delegates because they are either congressmen and senators or are high party officials.

Super Tuesday: The presidential primary election day in March when the most states hold their primaries and the most presidential convention delegates are up for grabs.

Target: To aim letters that deal with a specific issue, like mental health or clean water, only to the people who are likely to make a voting decision based on a candidate's position on that issue. That saves postage, and also shows the voter that a candidate knows what that voter cares about.

Targeted mail: Campaign mail aimed at people with a specific voting interest, like education, health care, or gun control.

Third party: A party formed in addition to the two major parties.

Third party candidate: A person who runs for office on a party that is neither the Republican nor the Democratic party.

Ticket: List of candidates of one party running in one election.

Ticket splitting: Dividing votes for different offices among different parties.

Top of the ticket: The person who is running for the most important job available in a particular election.

Unanimous: Voted for by everyone who is allowed to vote.

Uncommitted: Not pledged to any one candidate.

Uncontested: An election with only one candidate.

Unknown: Not famous.

Valid signatures: The names on a petition that have proven to be legitimate.

Volunteers: People who work without being paid.

Watergate Syndrome: The feeling that you can't trust people who are elected to office. The syndrome developed from the corruption that was revealed in the Watergate scandals in the Nixon administration of the early 1970s.

Winner-take-all: Circumstances where the winner of an election gets all the delegates or votes. The opposite would be a system that would give the winner the percentage he had won by, and the loser the rest.

Yellow-dog Democrat: A Democrat so loyal that he would elect Democratic candidates even if they were "yellow dogs."

Suggested Reading

Adult books are marked with an asterisk.

POLITICS

Archer, Jules. *Winners and Losers: How Elections Work in America*. San Diego: Harcourt Brace Jovanovich, 1984.

*Bernstein, Carl, and Bob Woodward. *All the President's Men*. New York: Simon and Schuster, 1974.

*Blumenthal, Sidney. *The Permanent Campaign*. New York: Simon and Schuster, 1983.

Broder, David S. *Changing of the Guard: Power and Leadership in America*. New York: Simon and Schuster, 1980.

Cook, Fred J. *American Political Bosses and Machines*. New York: Franklin Watts, 1973.

*Crouse, Timothy. *The Boys on the Bus*. New York: Ballantine, 1976.

Fradin, Dennis B. *Voting and Elections*. Chicago: Children's Press, 1985.

*Greenfield, Jeff. *Playing to Win*. New York: Simon and Schuster, 1980.

Haynes, Roy. *Political Campaigning*. New York: Franklin Watts, 1979.

Kronewetter, Michael. *Are You a Liberal, Are You a Conservative*. New York: Franklin Watts, 1984.

*McGinniss, Joe. *The Selling of the President, 1968*. New York: Pocket Books, 1984.

*Phillips, Kevin T. *The Emerging Republican Majority*. New York: Arlington House, 1969.

124

Plano, Jack C. *The American Political Dictionary.* New York: Henry Holt, 1985.

Priestly, E.J. *Finding Out About Elections.* Pomfret, Vt: David and Charles, 1983.

*Reeves, Richard. *Convention.* San Diego: Harcourt Brace Jovanovich, 1977.

*White, Theodore H. *The Making of the President, 1960.* New York: Atheneum, 1980.

GOVERNMENT

Beard, Charles A. *Charles A. Beard's The Presidents in American History.* New York: Messner, 1985.

Blassingame, Wyatt. *The Look-it-Up Book of Presidents.* New York: Random House, 1987.

Greene, Carol. *Congress.* Chicago: Children's Press, 1985.

Greene, Carol. *Presidents of the United States.* Chicago: Children's Press, 1984.

Liston, Robert. *We the People: Congressional Power.* New York: McGraw-Hill, 1975.

McCague, James. *The Office of President.* Easton, Md.: Garrard, 1975.

*O'Neill, Thomas P. *Man of the House.* New York: Random House, 1987.

*Schlesinger, Arthur M., Jr. *A Thousand Days.* Boston: Houghton-Mifflin, 1965.

PEOPLE

Ambrose, Stephen E. *Ike: Abilene to Berlin.* New York: Harper and Row, 1973.

*Cannon, Lou. *Reagan.* New York: Putnam, 1984.

Faber, Doris. *Eleanor Roosevelt: First Lady of the World.* New York: Puffin, 1986.

Fox, Mary Virginia. *Mister President: The Story of Ronald Reagan.* Hillside, NJ.: Enslow, 1986.

*Goodwin, Doris Kearns. *Lyndon Johnson and the American Dream.* New York: Signet, 1976.

Hargrove, Jim. *Dwight D. Eisenhower.* Encyclopedia of Presidents. Chicago: Children's Press, 1987.

*Lash, Joseph. *Eleanor and Franklin.* New York: Norton, 1971.

Lawson, Don. *Geraldine Ferraro: The Woman Who Changed American Politics.* New York: Messner, 1985.

Lawson, Don. *FDR's New Deal.* New York: Harper and Row, 1979.

Levy, Elizabeth, and Mara Miller. *Politicians for the People: Six Who Stand for Change.* New York: Dell, 1981.

*Miller, Merle. *Plain Speaking: An Oral Biograpy of Harry Truman.* New York: Berkley, 1986.

*Morris, Edmund. *The Rise of Teddy Roosevelt.* New York: Putnam, 1979.

Quackenbush, Robert M. *Don't You Dare Shoot That Bear: A Story of Theodore Roosevelt.* Englewood Cliffs, N.J.: Prentice-Hall, 1984.

Roberts, Naurice. *Barbara Jordan: The Great Lady From Texas.* Chicago: Children's Press, 1984.

Roberts, Naurice. *Henry Cisneros: Mexican-American Mayor.* Chicago: Children's Press, 1986.

*Schlesinger, Arthur M., Jr. *Robert Kennedy and His Times.* New York: Houghton Mifflin, 1978.

Smith, Betsy Covington. *Jimmy Carter, President.* New York: Walker and Co., 1986.

*Wills, Gary. *Nixon Agonistes.* New York: New American Library, 1979.

FICTION

Bradley, Virginia. *Who Could Forget the Mayor of Lodi?* New York: Dodd Mead, 1985.

*Drury, Alan. *Advise and Consent.* New York: Doubleday, 1959.

Kemp, Gene. *The Turbulent Term of Tyke Tiler.* London: Faber, 1980.

Kibbe, Pat. *My Mother, the Mayor, Maybe.* New York: Knopf, 1981.

Korman, Gordon. *Don't Care High.* New York: Scholastic, 1986.

Langton, Jane. *Fragile Flag.* New York: Harper and Row Junior Books, 1984.

Littke, Lael. *Trish for President.* San Diego: Harcourt Brace Jovanovich, 1984.

*O'Connor, Edwin. *The Last Hurrah.* New York: Bantam, 1970.

*Warren, Robert Penn: *All the King's Men.* New York: Random House, 1987.

MOVIES

You might want to rent or ask your teacher or family to rent one of these:

Mr. Smith Goes to Washington
Advise and Consent
All the King's Men
The Last Hurrah
The Candidate
Power
The Man
All the President's Men
State of the Union

Index